TARGET
U. S. A.

*The Inside Story of the
New Terrorist War*

LOUIS R. MIZELL, JR.

John Wiley & Sons, Inc.
New York • Chichester • Weinheim • Brisbane
Singapore • Toronto

Dedicated to the street police officer,
our first line of defense and the highest form
of law enforcement.

This book is printed on acid-free paper. ⊖

Copyright © 1998 by Louis R. Mizell, Jr. All rights reserved.

Published by John Wiley & Sons, Inc.

Published simultaneously in Canada.

This publication is designed to provide accurate and
authoritative information in regard to the subject matter
covered. It is sold with the understanding that the publisher
is not engaged in rendering legal, accounting, or other
professional services. If legal advice or other expert assistance
is required, the services of a competent professional person
should be sought.

Library of Congress Cataloging-in-Publication Data:

Mizell, Louis R.
    Target U.S.A.: the inside story of the new terrorist war / Louis R.
Mizell.
        p.   cm.
    Includes index.
    ISBN 0-471-17829-2 (cloth: alk. paper)
    1. Terrorism—United States.   2. Terrorism—United States—
Prevention.   3. Political violence—United States.   4. Internal
security—United States.   I. Title
HV6432.M58   1998
363.3'2'0973—dc21   97-49235
Printed in the United States of America.

10   9   8   7   6   5   4   3   2   1

Foreword

The Apostles of Power

W E LIVE IN NEW TIMES.
Deadly and confusing times.
Politics, business, and culture as mankind had defined such forces since the glory days of Athens evolved when the atomic fireball lit Hiroshima, when the gadget first used to broadcast images and sounds from Hitler's Olympic games became as common as indoor plumbing, when the first "ordinary individual" bought a computer linked to an invisible web of data bytes, when the last dot on a world map was defined so it could be fought over by institutionalized ideological armies. Somewhere in the nexus of these epic lightning bolts, we all became global dwellers—and we all became subject to the dangers of that passport, dangers increasingly personified in the violent apostles of power we call terrorists. In the preceding decade of your life, 35,000 Americans fell as direct victims of terrorism and political violence. All Americans paid involuntary tribute to terrorists through increased tax dollars and lost business revenue.

Consider yourself lucky: In our world where terrorists will do anything to advance an objective—no matter how seemingly bizarre—there are warriors like Lou Mizell who stand between them and you.

You may think you know about terrorists, but most of such wisdom probably comes from Hollywood movies, wonderful cultural fantasies that blur the scant knowledge you could have gleaned from thirty-second TV news stories, truncated newspaper prose, propaganda press-released by politicians, and misinformation spewed by self-labeled "experts" who see our rising tide of terror as a wave to surf towards lucrative celebrity shores. In our bold new world, the bombardment of data and information machine-gunned at us has actually decreased the depth of our knowledge and wounded our ability to put what we glimpse into perspective. The bullets keep coming, faster and faster until its all just a roar in which we "know" what we choose to believe.

Believe this: Terrorists are out there, and you are the means to their ends.

The two options you have are to trust in blind luck that you'll never be standing in an Atlanta mall when a terrorist goes for his gold, or to trust that knowing as much truth as you can will help you protect yourself and participate actively in your own triumphant survival as a businessperson, a voter, a taxpayer, a parent, a citizen.

Mizell and other intelligent, creative, brave warriors like him are your first line of defense against getting your legs blown off in a terrorist incident perpetrated by zealots you never knew existed. Unlike almost every other TV talk show "terrorist expert," Lou is an actual, flesh-and-blood operator who has real, not just academic, experience; a combat Marine Corps veteran of Vietnam; and a street veteran of the often invisible, deadly wars against political terrorists who target America and shed blood from Beirut to Boston.

Mizell has stepped beyond his strictly covert government service to battle terrorists by analyzing and countering their tactics, an example of privatization at its best. This rollercoaster book sandblasts a true picture of the foes you face, and will help you understand what to do the next time a politician or talk-show host asks for your dollars or your trust.

History is the biography of people who strive to foment—whether they are terrorists battling for some bloody cause, innocent victims struggling to survive, or warriors battling to save citizens who may not take the time to see what's happening around them until it's too late to do anything but perish and wonder why. This book is history.

Ironically, this book reads more like a page-turning thriller destined for the Hollywood screen than like history. And what emerges from the astounding, shocking, triumphant, and sometimes frustrating scenes in this history is that Mizell is not a lone hero; that hundreds of other American soldiers, agents, and police officers deserve glory for their silent and sometimes deadly sacrifices to keep us safe; that victims who refuse to let the horrors they've suffered give clean victory to the terrorists are involuntary but noble warriors in their own right.

Our lives are on the line in this new world without boundaries. Whether we like it or not, we must choose to fight, and to refuse to let terrorists become our only apostles of power.

JAMES GRADY
Former U.S. Senate Aide
Former investigative reporter for
    columnist Jack Anderson
Author, *Six Days of the Condor*

Acknowledgments

THIS BOOK, *TARGET U.S.A.,* IS THE RESULT OF THE cooperation of many unsung heros who banded together and enthusiastically shared their expertise, personal experiences, and energy. To this large group of professionals and patriots, I would like to say thank you. It is my firm belief that their efforts will help readers understand the real terrorist threat in the United States; their efforts will help save lives.

A special thank you to my brilliant and witty friend Ruth Ravenel, editor, writer, and Renaissance woman, whose valuable insights are imprinted on every page. Ruth, you have uncanny instincts and a wonderful soul; it is an honor to work with you.

When the going got tough my longtime friend, Jane Becker Garzilli, attorney, philosopher, consultant, stood by my side and didn't retreat an inch. Semper fi.

Becky Boyd, our loyal office manager, waved her magic wand and kept us all sane, productive, and organized. Your dedication, friendship, and professionalism are very much appreciated. Becky, you are the best.

Jennifer Pincott of John Wiley & Sons put her heart and soul into this book and believed in it from the beginning. You are a true professional. Thank you.

Acknowledgments

Attentive to every detail, Bernice Pettinato and Beehive Production Services proved they are the best in the business. Great job!

Jim Grady, my writing mentor, grabbed me by the collar and encouraged me to write this book. Thank you for your guidance, support, and adventures. Mark Olshaker and John Weisman, thanks for the inspiration.

Kevin Lamb, researcher, investigator, Marine, was able to uncover information others could not find. Great work!

Wise beyond her years, Ericka Walters has impressed us all with her discipline and hard work. Ericka, you are our future. A hug to you.

Pat B. Smith, businesswoman extraordinaire, equestrian, and good friend—thank you for being so positive and supportive. You are very special.

Inspector Don Moss and Detective Efrain "Freddie" Mendez of the NYPD, encyclopedias of terrorism knowledge, contributed valuable information. It was fun working with you.

Lisa Fentress, advisor, lawyer, writer; you never cease to amaze me. It's an honor to be associated with such a professional.

Patty Raine, artist, singer, soul mate—thank you, thank you, thank you. Victoria Brown Barquero, you did a terrific job. Jennifer Mar, your assistance was much appreciated.

Detectives Bill Cagney, Everett Obenhein, Chuck Peck, Steve Mayes, and Art Melandres, you were great partners. Bill Rathburn, law enforcement couldn't ask for a better representative.

Lieutenant Colonel Matt Tyszka, Connecticut State Police, and Don Feeney, former Delta Commando, I'm looking forward to many more adventures.

To nine special buddies on the Vietnam War Memorial, you were the best of the best.

After seventeen operations, my friend Alan Bigler, survivor of a Beirut embassy bombing, stands as the personification of grit and determination. Alan, you are an inspiration to all of us. Greg Bujac, William Clarke, and Bob O'Brian, you did it all. To Tony Deibler, my partner since Vietnam, congratulations on being the recipient of heroism awards in Bosnia, Monrovia, and Kuwait. Tim Dixon, Bill Trites, Chris Leibengood, Jim McWhirter, and Bill Penn, ain't life a wonderful adventure?! Dave Haas, philosopher, poet, agent; I'll never forget Nepal or Jordan. Sheri Mestan and Dennis Bochantin, you are a terrific team. To Bill Elderbaum, Rick Watts, Gary Saylor, Jeff Bozworth, Grace Goodier, Joan Lombardi, Steve Fakan, Bob Nuernberger, Bob Franks, Peter Roche, Carol Stricker, Allegra Sensenig, Dan McCarthy, Charlie Chase, Pat O'Hanlon, Larry Hartnett, Joan Andrews, Jim Hush, Liz Wood, John Murphy, Chris Andrews, Dennis Williams, Mike Crowe, Chris Riley, Dick Shoupe, Scott Tripp, Tony Bell, Bruce Tully, Pete Hargraves, Larry Liptak, and Beth Salamanca, and all the other unsung heros in the Diplomatic Security Service—it was an honor and great fun working with you.

Arleigh McCree, LAPD, Suzanne Conway, DSS, and Carl Shoffler, MPD, you are sadly missed.

A special salute to my friends and partners with the CIA, the FBI, the USSS, the DEA, the U.S. Marshals, the ATF, and the Delta Commandos, who contributed so much to this book. Thank you for being such dedicated warriors. Thank you for putting your lives on the line for America.

Finally, a bushel of carrots for a beautiful horse named "Buddy." I couldn't ask for a better friend or confidante.

LOUIS R. MIZELL, JR.

Contents

Contents

Contents

Introduction

S HORTLY BEFORE 9:00 A.M. ON A BEAUTIFUL SPRING day in 1995, twenty-one children under the age of five were finishing a snack in the day care center of Oklahoma City's Alfred P. Murrah Federal Building. At the time, Timothy J. McVeigh, a decorated, clean-cut Persian Gulf War veteran, allegedly pulled up to the front of the nine-story building in a yellow Ryder rental truck loaded with a massive bomb, turned off the truck's ignition, got out, and walked away. At 9:02 A.M., the 4,000 pounds of ammonium nitrate and diesel fuel detonated, disemboweling the Murrah building. The blast killed fifteen of the twenty-one children and maimed most of the other six. Eight law enforcement officers perished, as did mothers and fathers, sons and daughters, sisters and brothers. Timothy McVeigh was convicted of murdering 168 people and injuring more than 500 with a bomb that destroyed or damaged 312 surrounding offices, stores, and apartments.

The deadliest criminal act ever committed on U.S. soil showed Americans that even in our heartland, we are all vulnerable to terrorism. Many Americans still believe, however, that terrorism—the violence or threat of violence perpetrated by an individual or group for political, religious, or ideological reasons—plagues only other nations, places such as Jerusalem and Beirut, Belfast and London, Tokyo and Paris, Berlin and Bogotá. Not here, not in the United States, they think. Their perception is dead wrong.

Each of the 191 countries in the world has its own terrorist groups, most of which have operatives and sympathizers living in the United States. Iranians, Libyans, Palestinians, Armenians, Cubans, Croatians, Pakistanis, Indians, Japanese, Irish, Germans, Chileans, Chinese, Nicaraguans, Filipinos, and citizens of three dozen other countries have committed terrorist acts on U.S. soil. Scores of homegrown left- and right-wing American extremists also threaten our welfare and peace of mind. Throughout the past twenty years at least 128 domestic and international terrorist groups, plus state-directed intelligence services of a dozen rogue countries, have staged more than 3,150 violent incidents within our borders: politically motivated arsons, hijackings, armed robberies, bombings, kidnappings, hostage-takings, building takeovers, rampage shootings, and raids on armories, gun stores, and explosives storage sites.

Several groups have assaulted the Statue of Liberty because it is the most powerful symbol of American freedom. In 1965, Ray Wood and a group of other New York City intelligence officers arrested three men and a woman for plotting to blow up the icon of Ellis Island, the Washington Monument, and the Liberty Bell. They caught the conspirators while the quartet was transporting explosives from Canada to New York for the operation. On June 3, 1980, a bomb planted by the Croatian Freedom Fighters at the Statue of Liberty's base, exploded, causing significant damage but no injuries.

American citizens detonated a bomb at another symbolic site on November 7, 1983: the U.S. Capitol. The Armed Resistance Unit, as they called themselves, said they were protesting U.S. imperialism in Lebanon, Grenada, El Salvador, and Nicaragua. No one was hurt. A few weeks earlier, U.S. Capitol

Police had arrested Israeli citizen Israel Rubinowitz in the public gallery above the U.S. House of Representatives. He was wearing a bogus body bomb beneath his coat and threatened to "blow us up." He was deported.

Using bullets, bombs, knives, and other lethal weapons, diverse terrorist groups operating inside the United States, including dozens of native-born Americans, attempted or successfully carried out more than 250 assassinations. Haitian terrorists opposed to ousted-President Jean-Bertrand Aristide, for example, gunned down four Miami-based pro-Aristide radio show hosts and political activists between 1991 and 1994. American intelligence agents uncovered a handwritten hit list with the names of exiled Haitian journalists, including all four of the murder victims, that read: "This is a list of people in Haiti, Miami, and Canada who must be executed before the 30th of October 1993." Haitian military leaders had reluctantly agreed to permit Aristide to return from exile and be reinstated as president on that date.

More than a dozen Vietnamese writers and activists have been assassinated in the United States. On August 19, 1989, in Fresno, California, Doan Van Toai, executive director of the Institute for Democracy in Vietnam (IDV), was shot to death by two unknown Asian men. In Virginia, on September 22, 1990, Mr. Triet Le, an anticommunist writer for the Vietnamese newspaper *Tien Phong,* and his wife, Tuyet Thi Dangturn, were both gunned down in the carport of their home.

Between 1970 and 1981, the Taiwanese Independence Movement (TIM) assassinated the brother-in-law of the mayor of Kaohsiung, Taiwan, Li Chiang-Lin in Los Angeles; probably assassinated scholar Cho Ren Wu at the University of Maryland; and attempted to assassinate Chiang Ching-Kuo, a son of dictator Chiang Kai-Shek, at Manhattan's posh Plaza Hotel. The Taiwan intelligence service ordered the October 15, 1984, murder of Henry Liu, a Chinese-American author and critic of the Taiwan regime, in Dale City, California.

An Armenian terrorist killed two Turkish diplomats in 1973 at a Santa Barbara hotel. Two assassins approached the car of Turkish Consul General Kemal Arikan from two different directions at 9:50 A.M. on January 28, 1982. Arikan had stopped his car at the intersection of Wilshire Boulevard and Comstock Avenue in Westwood, California. They shot him, fatally. Arikan did not use the two Turkish bodyguards assigned to him because he feared for their safety should an assassination attempt against him occur.

Members of a Venezuelan death squad allegedly shot and killed Ernesto Diaz Rohn, a Venezuelan dissident, in Fort Lauderdale, Florida, on November 2, 1980. Sikh extremists shot and killed an Indian government employee, his wife, and a relative in Tacoma, Washington, on August 1, 1984.

Three gunmen stormed into the Miami home of Nicaraguan General Reinaldo Perez-Vega's widow on January 29, 1983. When Perez-Vega's eight-year-old son pleaded with the terrorists, "Don't hurt my mommy," they shot the child in the head, killing him. Mrs. Vega feigned death after being shot three times. Several years earlier, in Nicaragua, notorious Sandanista rebel Nora Astorga lured the top Somoza general to her bedroom for an assignation but he was met with assassination. As Astorga caressed her enemy, another waiting rebel slit his throat.

Institutions of higher education have served both as hiding places for terrorists and targets. Alluring assassin Nora Astorga was once a student at Catholic University in Washington, D.C. Another terrorist, Rose Dugdale, who bombed and kidnapped for the Irish Republican Army, attended Mount Holyoke College in Massachusetts. Animal rights groups—going by such names as Animal Liberation Front, Band of Mercy, Urban Gorillas, and Animal Rights Militia—have attacked numerous universities and colleges in the United States. In 1987, the Animal Liberation Front burned down a laboratory at the University of California at Davis causing $3.5 million in damages.

In 1992, animal activists set fire to a lab at Michigan State University causing $125,000 in damages and destroying thirty-two years of research using minks.

And in the early morning chill of February 26, 1993, a group of Middle Eastern terrorists loaded 1,200 pounds of explosives into a Ryder rental van and drove the vehicle to a hotel parking garage beneath the World Trade Center. As 50,000 office workers went about their daily routines, the powerful bomb detonated, killing 6 people and injuring more than 1,000. The blast shattered one tower of the 110-story symbol of Western wealth, power, and capitalism, and destroyed the illusion that American citizens on U.S. soil were immune to foreign terrorism.

Central Intelligence Agency Director John Deutch warned Congress on February 22, 1996, that terrorism will increasingly threaten the United States. At that hearing, Deutch also announced that many rogue countries, such as Iran, Iraq, North Korea, and Libya, and several anti-American, subnational (anti-regime) groups are acquiring weapons of mass destruction: nuclear, chemical, and biological.

When I returned from Vietnam in 1969, a very difficult time in my life and in America, I had a recurring dream that endless waves of enemy soldiers were attacking me. Despite the wounding of some members of my entrenched squad, none of us was fearful of being overrun; no matter how many times the enemy laid siege, we prevented them from gaining any ground. The most confusing aspect of the dream was that the fruitless battle never ended. We would think the fight was over, but the attackers kept relentlessly charging and charging and charging.

After being released from the Marine Corps and earning a master's degree in law enforcement from the American University, I was recruited by the Office of Diplomatic Security of the U.S. Department of State. I had the highly unusual position of being both a special agent and an intelligence analyst.

In addition to assignments to protect and investigate, which took me to 105 countries, my mission was to monitor more than 100 terrorist groups operating inside the United States. The post-Vietnam nightmares eventually stopped, but in my new profession, a new enemy continuously charged, changed face, and charged again.

I resigned from government service in 1988 to start an international security firm that chases fugitives, does international troubleshooting, and specializes in intelligence data not retrievable from other sources. My company produces databases on 4,000 categories of crime and terrorism. I have discovered that, with the Cold War over, the single greatest threat to the United States is the terror from within, from those who commit indiscriminate murder—murderers such as whoever planted the July 27, 1996, bomb at the Atlanta Summer Olympics that killed a woman and caused the fatal heart attack of a foreign correspondent. *Target U.S.A.* is about the terrorists who want to destroy America and the law enforcement personnel who have sworn to protect the greatest country in the world.

* * *

All of the assassinations, bombings, and other terrorist incidents in this book are well documented and, to the best of my knowledge, are true and factual. In the interests of privacy and national security, a few names and operational details have been changed.

CHAPTER

1

Cloak and Dagger

What the Public Doesn't See

A N ARMED MAN AND WOMAN, WEARING WIGS AND eyeglasses with plain lenses, loaded an Uzi submachine gun, a shotgun, and 672 pounds of volatile explosives into a public storage locker in Cherry Hill, New Jersey. Susan Lisa Rosenberg, twenty-nine, and Timothy Blunk, twenty-seven, both members of the May 19 Communist Organization, a group closely linked to the Weather Underground Organization (WUO), had used false identification to rent the space. Cherry Hill police officers Mark DeFrancisco and Craig Martin arrested the pair at the scene on November 29, 1984, confiscated the cache, and also found maps showing armored car routes and phony identification documents for posing as police and Federal Bureau of Investigation (FBI) agents. It took police a day to determine the pair's real names and that they were wanted for murder, armored car robbery, a violent prison escape, and a $31,000 armed robbery in Connecticut. The 672 pounds of explosives had been stolen in Austin, Texas in 1980.

Although terrorists waged more than 3,150 terrorist operations in the United States from January 1977 to January

1998, the particulars are not widely known. The primary reason: a lot of terrorism is invisible. The police and the press record and report as so-called common crimes the hundreds of incidents each year that domestic and international terrorist groups perpetrate in this country. A wide range of circumstances affect public perception of terrorism. When terrorists don't claim responsibility for a shooting, a robbery, or a bombing, as often happens, it appears that we have less terrorism than is actually occurring. The public may hear a news story about the incident but they do not associate the crime with terrorism, especially long after the fact.

Another problem is that law enforcement often doesn't find out until months or years later that a particular incident was perpetrated by terrorists. By that time, the public has completely forgotten about the shooting, bombing, or robbery. Rosenberg's and Blunk's crimes are cases in point. Except for a relatively few interested parties, who remembers them?

For citizens to accurately gauge the terrorist threat, they need to know about both the incidents that actually happened and the terrorist attacks that law enforcement prevented.

During the past twenty years, dozens of terrorist organizations have robbed at least 368 banks and armored cars. These groups include the Puerto Rican Armed Forces of National Liberation, or FALN for Fuerzas Armadas de Liberacion Nacional, and Macheteros organizations, the Black Liberation Army (BLA), the WUO, the Sam Melville–Jonathan Jackson Brigade, and at least fifteen separate right-wing militia groups. The right-wing neo-Nazi group, The Order, attacked armored bank vehicles in Ukiah, California, and Seattle, Washington, netting $4 million for the extremists.

During 1996 and 1997, law enforcement authorities thwarted more than two dozen terrorist attacks in the United States; none has had the impact on the American public as has the Oklahoma City bombing—nor should they. But serious danger lurks.

Authorities arrested seven men from West Virginia, Ohio, and Pennsylvania with ties to the paramilitary group, Mountaineer Militia, who were plotting to blow up the FBI's Criminal Justice Information Services fingerprint facility in Clarksburg, West Virginia. According to FBI affidavits, the Mountaineer Militia had also pondered assassinating Senator John D. Rockefeller and Federal Reserve Chairman Alan Greenspan in a "holy war" against the federal government. The right-wing extremists maintained that the assassinations would not be murder because the militia was fighting government corruption.

Three Idaho militiamen were convicted on July 23, 1997, in Spokane, Washington, of two bank robberies and three bombings. The militiamen sometimes used diversionary bombs to distract the police, detonating one outside the *Spokane Review* newspaper office moments before robbing and bombing a U.S. Bank branch on April 1, 1996. They bombed a Planned Parenthood office on July 12, 1996, shortly before robbing the U.S. Bank again. The militiamen netted $108,000 in the two robberies, which has never been recovered.

The three men, all from Sandpoint, Idaho, testified that they were an antigovernment militia cell whose members believe that usury is evil and punishable by death. They consider themselves "Ambassadors of Yaweh" (Yaweh is the Hebrew word for God in the Old Testament of the Bible) and believe that Northern Europeans are the true Israelites.

Law enforcement officials in five states—Missouri, Wisconsin, Texas, Colorado, and Kansas—coordinated efforts to prevent massacres at military installations in the United States, starting with Fort Hood in Killeen, Texas, during Fourth of July celebrations.

At 6:15 A.M. on July 4, 1997, authorities crept into a campsite at a state park in San Saba County, Texas, and arrested two heavily armed militiamen. Undercover police officers learned that the two men were part of a group that had planned to massacre foreign troops at U.S. military installations. Five other men and women involved in the same scheme were arrested in Wisconsin and Kansas.

Members of the bizarre militia group, which has no name, erroneously believed that United Nations troops were being housed at U.S. military bases in preparation for the imposition of a world police force and a sinister New World Order.

Weapons confiscated from the seven would-be terrorists included handguns, a machine gun, 1,600 rounds of ammunition, ten pipe bombs, rolls of cannon fuse, mysterious chemicals, silencers, a night-vision scope, and bullet-resistant vests.

On October 20, 1981, members of five domestic terrorist organizations attacked a Brink's armored car in Nanuet, New York. The terrorists killed a Brink's guard and two policemen and fled with $1,589,000 in cash. Police later learned that the same terrorists had robbed at least five other armored bank vehicles, killing two guards and wounding another. Statisticians tallying up the number of people killed in the United States by terrorists usually fail to include the many men and women who die during robberies probably committed to support terrorist activities.

Three men and one woman, all members of the True Knights of the Ku Klux Klan, allegedly plotted to place bombs at a gas refinery as a diversionary tactic so they could then more easily rob an armored car of $2 million during the chaos. They planned to time some of the bombs to detonate and kill police as the officers arrived on the scene. The FBI arrested the four suspects on April 22, 1997, in Fort Worth, Texas, before their plot unfolded.

Prison escapes are another form of invisible terrorism. Joanne Chesimard, the soul of the Black Liberation Army, escaped from prison in New Jersey with the help of three accomplices who brandished weapons and took hostages. The twice-wounded revolutionary, who is still at large, had been serving a life sentence for murdering one New Jersey police officer and wounding another.

In 1995 two former WUO members went to prison for plotting to blast FALN leader Oscar Lopez out of Leavenworth Federal Penitentiary. The plot called for blowing up the maximum security prison, landing a helicopter, and shooting guards.

There have been at least sixty-one dramatic prison escapes and attempted escapes by terrorist groups in the United States, resulting in many deaths, injuries, and hostage-takings. But since prison escapes are usually recorded and publicized as common crime, the public does not often perceive them as terrorism.

On September 20, 1970, two seniors at Brandeis University, Katherine Ann Power and Susan Saxe, joined up with three former prison inmates and raided the National Guard armory in Newburyport, Massachusetts. They stole a pickup truck, blasting caps, and 400 rounds of .30-caliber ammunition. Three days later, the same group robbed the State Street Bank and Trust Company in Boston and murdered Walter Schroeder, a forty-two-year-old Boston police officer.

Power was one of the most sought-after female fugitives in U.S. history, remaining underground for twenty-three years until her attorneys negotiated her surrender to authorities in 1993.

From 1970 to 1997 armed terrorists have raided at least 122 armories, weapons stores, and explosives storage sites in the United States. The weapons and explosives stolen have wounded or killed more than 200 people and have caused tens of millions of dollars in damages. Although these violent robberies are clearly terrorist operations, they often go unrecognized as such.

And in literally hundreds of unsolved cases we may never know whether an incident was politically motivated. In 1986, Ismail Al-Faruqi, a Palestinian religious scholar and professor of religion at Temple University, and his wife were murdered in their Philadelphia home. Was he assassinated for political reasons? Possibly, but we don't know for sure.

On January 23, 1996, in Miami, Gouquiang Situ, a forty-year-old recent Chinese immigrant, stepped on a trip wire at a bus stop and triggered an explosion that literally blew his head off. Was that terrorism? No group has claimed responsibility.

In Los Angeles two days later, police found Dr. Haing S. Ngor shot to death in front of his Chinatown home. Dr. Ngor won an Academy Award for his role as a fellow Cambodian in the 1984 movie, *The Killing Fields*. Was Dr. Ngor, who had been tortured by the Khmer Rouge, a victim of terrorism as many in the Cambodian community have suggested? Murder charges were filed against three Asian men whom police believe committed the murder during a robbery. But as a Cambodian activist stated: "Many political assassinations of Cambodians and Vietnamese in the United States are made to look like robbery."

Good security, good intelligence, aggressive law enforcement, and a lot of luck have prevented hundreds of terrorist incidents over the years. If the perpetrators had been more successful, the public would have an entirely different perception of the terrorist reality in the United States.

A few days before Easter in 1995, authorities apprehended two Japanese travelers at Los Angeles International Airport who had allegedly planned a toxic nerve gas attack at Disneyland theme park in Anaheim, California. Japanese police alerted the FBI earlier in the month that the two men were members of the cult Aum Supreme Truth and were flying to the United States. Aum Supreme Truth is the cult that released sarin, a poison gas, into a Tokyo subway system, killing twelve people and sickening thousands of others. The two terrorists had planned to release the gas during the nightly fireworks display at the amusement park when attendance typically swelled to maximum capacity.

President Clinton cited the incident as an example of the sort of counterterrorist activity by the federal government that "the public does not see, most of which I should not comment on."

CHAPTER

A Far-Reaching Hand

Trouble from Abroad

O N APRIL 27, 1980, COLONEL MOAMMAR QADDAFI commanded all Libyan dissidents living abroad—or "stray dogs," as he called them—to return to Libya or be liquidated. By the end of 1980, Libyan hit teams had assassinated ten Libyan exiles living in Italy, Great Britain, Greece, and Germany.

As previously mentioned, terrorism is often defined as violence or the threat of violence perpetrated by an individual or group for political, religious, or ideological reasons. From 1977 to January 1998 at least 128 domestic and foreign terrorist organizations committed some form of political, religious, or ideological violence in the United States. Approximately 95 of these groups, and all 18 groups espousing Middle Eastern or Islamic causes, have enlisted and deployed American citizens in some or all of their operations. Libya's Colonel Qaddafi has cleverly recruited former Central Intelligence Agency (CIA) agents and U.S. military personnel, American Black Muslims, and even a Chicago street gang to do his bidding in the United States.

Faisal Zagallai, a thirty-five-year-old graduate student at Colorado State University in Fort Collins, was one of 10,000

Libyans residing in the United States in 1980 and was an out-spoken critic of Qaddafi. Along with twenty-three other Libyan students studying in the United States, the Libyan dictator marked Zagallai for death. At Qadaffi's behest, an intelligence officer at Libya's embassy in Washington, D.C., contacted a Libyan college student who was a hard-core member of one of twenty Libyan Revolutionary Committees with networks throughout the United States. American intelligence quickly learned that "revolutionary committee" was a euphemism for "assassination squad."

Intensely loyal to Qaddafi, the college student consulted with a one-time Green Beret to find a hit man for the job. The ex-Green Beret—a former instructor at ex-CIA operative Frank Terpil's terrorist school—recruited his jobless American buddy, Eugene Aloys Tafoya, for the Zagallai job.

The Libyan government abruptly ended Zagallai's scholarship and cut off all financial assistance. Without financial aid, Zagallai and his wife Farida, a Ph.D. in sociology, were dependent on part-time jobs to survive.

On October 13, 1980, the Zagallais received a telephone call from a well-spoken woman, claiming to be a representative of IBM. The woman explained that IBM needed people to translate technical manuals from English to Arabic. The company was offering $2,000 per month. "Would you and your wife be interested in interviewing for this position?" the polite woman asked. Strapped for cash, Zagallai replied, "Yes, we're very interested."

The Zagallais arranged to meet with a recruiter the following evening.

As Zagallai hung up the phone, Farida nervously asked, "Do you think this could be a plot by Qaddafi?"

"It could be," Zagallai replied, "but I've got my gun." It didn't occur to the Zagallais to call IBM and verify the authenticity of the recruiter, and the couple was unaware that Qaddafi's operatives had used the "employment interview" tactic in the past. They also assumed that any would-be assassins would be Arabs.

At 7:00 P.M. on October 14, the American "corporate recruiter" for IBM knocked at the Zagallais' door and they welcomed him into their living room. At the time Farida wondered why, after ten minutes of chatting awkwardly, the man had not asked any relevant questions. She later recalled that the well-dressed, middle-aged man appeared nervous and smelled of alcohol.

From the kitchen, where she had gone to pour a glass of orange juice for the recruiter, she heard her husband shout, "It's him, Farida!" and then three gun shots. The recruiter had suddenly stood up, delivered a karate chop to Zagallai and opened fire. Farida ran to the bedroom, tried to jump out of the ground-floor window, and screamed for help. The recruiter, Eugene Tafoya, fled the scene.

Farida found her husband lying unconscious on the living room floor. He had retrieved his handgun from beneath a couch cushion but had had no time to use it. Although Zagallai survived the attack, one .22-caliber bullet passed through his skull, severed an optic nerve, and left him blind in one eye. A second bullet entered his right temple and remains lodged near his palate. The third round, fired at a range of three feet, missed Zagallai completely.

Qaddafi had reached out from Libya and recruited an American citizen, paying him to silence a political foe in a quiet American college town.

Eugene Tafoya falsified his birth certificate when he was fifteen years old to join the U.S. Marine Corps. By the time he retired in 1976, he was a decorated twenty-three-year veteran of both the Korean conflict and the Vietnam War, where he served as a Green Beret in the U.S. Army. Eleven years before retiring, he reportedly chastised his company commander for not supplying air cover that might have saved many lives when his company was under Viet Cong attack. The Army court-martialed the Bronze Star winner for being disrespectful to an officer and demoted him from sergeant to private.

For several months after the attempted assassination, Fort Collins police could not develop any leads. Their fortune changed in February 1981. Two boys playing in an irrigation ditch a mile from the Zagallais' home found a .22-caliber handgun, its serial numbers still intact.

Police traced the gun to a pawnshop in Fayetteville, North Carolina—the home of Fort Bragg and the Green Berets. The pawnshop had sold the gun to Tully Francis Strong who told investigators that he later sold it to his friend, Eugene Aloys Tafoya.

I knew Tafoya to be a very heavy drinker and a blowhard who was hardly the skilled, highly trained hitman he professed to be. On the day of the bungled assassination, Tafoya rented a car in his own name from Dollar Rent-a-Car at the Denver Airport. Once investigators had the murder weapon, they simply followed a trail of motel receipts, credit card records, telephone calls, bank deposits, and passport entries directly to Truth or Consequences, New Mexico. There they arrested Tafoya.

When Federal Bureau of Investigation (FBI) agents searched Tafoya's modest stucco home they discovered, among other things, a copy of *The Green Book* by Qaddafi, which outlines the dictator's political and social philosophy; Libyan currency; a Kuwaiti driver's license; and evidence that he had been working and training in Libya. They also found a hit list naming not Libyan dissidents, but American citizens.

In Truth or Consequences the FBI uncovered intriguing evidence that Tafoya was closely linked to fugitives Edwin Wilson and Frank Terpil. As a covert operative for the CIA, Terpil had helped organize the disastrous Bay of Pigs invasion by anti-Castro Cubans in 1961. Terpil and his colleague Wilson were renegade intelligence agents who popped through the veneer of secrecy, and both men signed on with Moammar

Qaddafi. A federal grand jury indicted them on charges of illegally selling weapons and explosives to Qaddafi, recruiting other former CIA agents and U.S. servicemen to train terrorists in Libya and setting up "hit squads" to assassinate enemies of Libya worldwide. (In 1981, reliable sources also told me that Libya had recruited forty-three Americans to help train Palestinian guerrillas in Libya, information that was later confirmed.) The grand jury also indicted Terpil and his wife Marilyn on charges of selling arms to President Idi Amin of Uganda, who exercised a genocidal reign of terror on his own people before fleeing to Libya for sanctuary.

Instead of fighting the predators who were stalking Americans worldwide, Wilson and Terpil used their CIA training and contacts to support our enemies—and themselves. Training and arming the international terrorist community, and thereby selling out America, made the two fugitives filthy rich. In 1981 Wilson was living a lavish lifestyle in Libya, and Terpil was hiding out in Beirut in an apartment overlooking the Mediterranean Sea. Most of Wilson's assistants in Libya, where he was safe from extradition by the U.S. government, were American Vietnam veterans.

One of the veterans whom Wilson recruited to instruct Libyan commando teams was John Dutcher, a tough ex-Marine who had earned black belts in three styles of the martial arts. He was also a gourmet chef of Korean cuisine. When Wilson became an international fugitive, Dutcher became his bodyguard. The news saddened me greatly because Dutcher had been one of my early karate instructors when he ran a school in Bethesda, Maryland.

Wilson was eventually caught, and a judge sentenced him to fifty-two years in prison for selling twenty-two tons of C-4 explosives and illegal arms to Libya, in addition to the attempted murder of two federal prosecutors and six other people. He resides in the maximum security prison of Marion, Ohio.

Terpil is still at large.

After the 1980 shooting of Faisal Zagallai, Tafoya traveled to southern England where he spent a leisurely month at a seventeenth-century farm estate owned by Wilson. Tafoya's personal papers, confiscated by the FBI, listed the private telephone and telex numbers for Wilson in Tripoli.

Tafoya's neighbors told investigators that he frequently disappeared for long periods of time and always returned with a bundle of money. My Middle Eastern sources had been telling me for years that Qaddafi pays his foreign mercenaries huge sums of cash for terrorist activities.

A judge ruled that much of the prosecution's evidence implicating Tafoya as an operative of the Libyan dictator was "not directly relevant to the shooting." The jury never heard it, and the case turned into a routine felony trial. On January 5, 1982, the trial judge sentenced Tafoya to two years' imprisonment for third-degree assault and six months for conspiracy.

The assassination attempt against Faisal Zagallai by an American in America galvanized the Reagan Administration, which reacted by closing the Libyan embassy or "People's Bureau" as the Libyans called it, and expelling twenty-seven Libyan diplomats. Despite the closure, Qaddafi continued ordering mercenaries and U.S.-based Libyans to do his bidding.

Two months after President Ronald Reagan closed the Libyan embassy, Libyan national Mohammed Shabata shot fellow student and countryman Nabil A. Mansour five times at close range with a .22-caliber handgun. Police found Mansour's bullet-riddled body inside his car's trunk in Ogden, Utah. They arrested the assassin at Chicago's O'Hare Airport as he boarded a flight to London en route to Libya.

Shabata had returned to Libya a year earlier for "training" but his classmate Mansour had refused to accompany him. Mansour, by virtue of doing nothing, became a "stray dog."

On May 19, 1984, the FBI arrested two Libyan intelligence officers posing as students in Philadelphia after they bought handguns and silencers from an FBI undercover agent. Without question, the undercover operation prevented assassinations in the United States. Both men were convicted and sent to prison.

Another Libyan intelligence officer, Muhammad Abdalla, posed as a college student to gain entry into the United States. When he learned that U.S. intelligence operatives had uncovered his true mission here—to assassinate anti-Qaddafi activists—and that he was about to be arrested, he fled the country.

Angry that American undercover officers were arresting his would-be assassins, Qaddafi tried another tactic: He recruited a Chicago street gang and a Japanese terrorist group.

In the early 1970s, Jeff Fort, who led a Chicago street gang called the Blackstone Rangers, went to prison for misapplying federal funds earmarked for an inner-city job training program. Fort converted to Islam while in prison, and, after his release, he changed the name of his old gang to El Rukns, which means "the foundation" in Arabic. Fort claimed that the group was a religious organization working to improve the black community. Prosecutors eventually charged the El Rukn "religious" group with twenty-three murders, several kidnappings, and a long list of drug-dealing and prostitution offenses.

Considered one of the first corporate-style supergangs, the well-organized El Rukns recognized that terrorism could be a lucrative financial venture. And who better to sponsor this venture than Moammar Qaddafi. The El Rukns sought out representatives of the Libyan government and worked out a business deal with Qaddafi. In exchange for $2.5 million, the gang agreed to commit terrorist acts in the United States.

Fortunately, American intelligence agents intervened. Working in conjunction with numerous federal, state, and local law enforcement agencies, the FBI arrested several members of the El Rukns on August 5, 1986, and charged them with weapon violations and conspiracy to carry out terrorist attacks in exchange for money from Libya. Raids on the group's hideouts yielded an M-72 antitank weapon and forty-one handguns and rifles, including three fully automatic shoulder weapons. Jeff Fort and other El Rukn members went to jail but others, such as Melvin Mays, became fugitives. Some El Rukn members who are believed to have traveled to Libya are still at large.

Jeff Fort's conversion to Islam while in prison is not unusual. Prison officials allow members of diverse religious groups to enter correctional facilities for the legitimate purpose of teaching the tenets of their faiths. In the United States, politics and religion don't mix, shouldn't mix, and, by constitutional law, they can't mix. Yet some "scholars," principally members of the Islamic Guerillas of America (IGA), have legally gone into U.S. prisons to teach Islam but instead have used the forum to preach politics, turning American jails into terrorist recruitment centers.

I heard one such "scholar" call the inmates "political prisoners" and criticize the "barbaric" conditions of American prisons, earning applause from his captive audiences. If these same inmates had committed their crimes—rape, armed robbery, murder, and drug trafficking—in Iran, instead of being incarcerated, they may well have been executed, with or without a trial. And if they had been incarcerated, they probably would have wished they'd been executed. I've seen Iranian jails; they aren't pretty.

Hoping to create chaos and revolution in the United States, some Middle Eastern leaders have fanned the flames of racism. Addressing a Nation of Islam convention held in Chicago in 1985, Libyan leader Moammar Qaddafi urged blacks and Native Americans "to create a sovereign and independent state in America," and offered to train and arm them. He suggested that the 400,000 blacks now in the U.S. armed services form the core resistance.

America has serious social problems, but neither the nations that propagate terrorism nor the Ayatollah Khomeinis, Saddam Husseins, or Moammar Qaddafis of the world cares one iota about U.S. social ills or has American interests at heart.

Purporting sympathy for the downtrodden and cynically and condescendingly presenting themselves as saviors, the IGA leadership's secret agenda began to crystallize: exploiting disaffected Americans to do their terrorist dirty work. I concluded this long before overhearing an intimate conversation between two of Khomeini's intelligence officers. The two men publicly professed solidarity with African-Americans but privately described blacks in the most demeaning and derogatory manner. "Violence comes naturally to the blacks," one Iranian intelligence officer averred. "They can be valuable in eliminating our enemies."

Pretending to be saviors, the intelligence officers were clearly using religion as a political tool and were playing young black men as suckers.

CHAPTER 3

To Know
Your Enemy

Lessons from Practice

CASUALLY POINTING TO A PARTIALLY DISSECTED female cadaver, the grandmotherly anatomy professor looked in my direction and asked, "Seat number 89. What gland is responsible for the lubrication of the vagina during the sexual response?"

I had seen a lot of dead and mutilated people in my career, but I had never seen a corpse in a classroom. And never in my graduate or undergraduate courses in criminal justice and psychology had a teacher asked me such an indelicate question.

Feigning to be a first-year student at the prestigious medical school, I answered as best I could: "I'm sorry, I couldn't hear the question." I was stalling for time. I'd chosen a seat in the last upper tier of seats, hoping to remain inconspicuous, but still able to keep an eye on Shadia, my protectee.

Shadia was the twenty-three-year-old daughter of a very high-ranking Middle Eastern official. Although enrolled in a London medical school, she was studying in the United States for one semester while her mother "secretly" underwent treatment for an undisclosed ailment. Within a month of Shadia's and her mother's arrival in America, individuals claiming to represent the Jewish Defense League (JDL) delivered threats to the two women.

Hardened by terrorism in her own country, Shadia initially ignored the menacing telephone calls and attended to her studies. But then unknown persons "Helter-Skeltered" her off-campus apartment: throwing blood on the walls and leaving a rifle cartridge on her bedroom pillow. Shadia was rightfully frightened and called her father.

I had protected "The Minister," as I called him, the previous year at the United Nations General Assembly in New York. Although the State Department regarded him as "high risk"—he barely survived two attempts on his life—The Minister remained nonchalant, even complacent about his own security. The gentle man once told me: "I'd feel terrible guilt and sorrow if you or your agents got hurt protecting me." Since we had all protected arrogant SOBs who considered us no more than expendable peons and servants, we greatly appreciated his sentiment. I genuinely liked and respected the man.

The Minister's attitude toward his daughter's security, however, was wholly different.

At midnight, just minutes after receiving the call from Shadia, The Minister broke protocol and called me at home. Considering that my rank was considerably below his, I didn't work for his government, and my number was unlisted, his calling me was highly unusual.

"Are you familiar with the tactics of the Jewish Defense League?" he inquired.

One aspect of my job with the State Department was to follow all terrorist organizations operating in the United States; my specialty was terrorist tactics. The JDL is an American terrorist organization that preaches "Death to Arabs" and is responsible for dozens of lethal bombings, arsons, and assassinations inside and outside the United States. Despite my personal respect for The Minister, I had to be careful not to reveal too much information about my sources and capabilities.

In the intelligence business, all countries are potential enemies. While the United States provides vast amounts of intelligence information to our foreign allies, American agents must tactfully treat every foreign country and its citizens as potential espionage threats. Israel, France, and Japan are among our closest friends and allies, but all three countries have used spies to steal our most sensitive, top-secret intelligence—thefts that have greatly hurt the United States. I had worked with Jonathan Jay Pollard, a U.S. naval intelligence officer who was caught passing classified information to Israel, the single largest recipient of U.S. financial aid and support. We all felt angry and betrayed by Pollard and by Israel. American taxpayers, of all religions, had generously given hundreds of billions of dollars to a country that stole our classified defense intelligence.

Cutting to the chase, The Minister explained that alleged Jewish extremists had threatened his daughter and asked whether I would protect her. I said I would be honored to take the assignment but explained that I did not have the authority to accept. His request, I told him, "would receive the utmost consideration." I hated myself for sounding like a federal bureaucrat. "It might take some time," I said apologetically.

"We'll see about that."

Two hours later I was en route to medical school with a small, hand-picked, highly trained protection team. I later learned that The Minister's next call had been to his good friend, the president of the United States.

I had been Shadia's bodyguard for two weeks when her well-regarded medical professor put me on the spot. She impatiently repeated the question about a specific female gland, a bit louder this time, but now ninety-three students had turned around in their chairs and were staring up at me.

"I don't know," I responded, somewhat befuddled.

Shadia glanced back at me with an impish look on her face. We had grown to like each other.

"May-I-ask-why-you-don't-know?!" the no-nonsense professor bellowed. A State Department agent on my team later joked that I looked more uncomfortable than the cadaver.

"I didn't study the lesson," I immediately regretted saying.

"Well then, perhaps you should stop wasting my time and your money and find a new profession!" the professor counseled coldly.

Shadia, who could barely contain her amusement, inadvertently attracted the professor's attention.

"Seat number 51. Please give us the answer so we can move on."

"The gland responsible for the lubrication of the vagina during the sexual response is the Bartholin gland." Shadia had correctly answered the question in her mesmerizing, part Arabic, part French, and part British accent.

"Correct!" praised the professor.

Chancing a glance back at me, Shadia smiled brilliantly and I gave her a "thumbs-up," which I knew she would interpret as congratulations.

When my team and I were satisfied that the good professor was not one of about 260 educators in the United States who were known to be members of extremist organizations, we took her aside, briefed her on the threat to Shadia and informed her that I was not a student. "Well, I hope I didn't discourage you from becoming a doctor," she said, laughing uproariously.

Although Shadia and I were from completely different cultures, we did have one thing in common: callers alleging to be with the Jewish Defense League had threatened each of us. They targeted Shadia because she was, by virtue of birth, a high-profile Arab and because her country had the audacity to discuss peace and compromise with Israel, an option the JDL opposed. Just like some Palestinian terrorist groups, the JDL has detonated bombs and killed people, hoping to derail the peace process.

The JDL threatened me because I testified against them in court during a case that involved a series of murders, bombings, and arsons. My hang-up caller, presumably an American citizen, either didn't know or care that I had risked my life protecting Israeli officials, had lectured to New York synagogues on how to defend themselves against Arab terrorists, and had frequently teamed up with Israeli intelligence, military, and law enforcement personnel.

In my court appearance I had detailed harassments, beatings, bombings, and torchings that the JDL had inflicted upon dozens of Soviet diplomats, musicians, dancers, and athletes when they visited the United States. The Soviet and international media accurately reported these menacing and embarrassing incidents that not only made all Americans look like thugs and terrorists but also, ironically, helped foster and justify anti-Semitism in Russia. When I was in Moscow organizing security arrangements for a visit by the U.S. secretary of state, one of my Russian counterparts told me that American terrorists had blown up his car and had fired four bullets through his office window when he was assigned to New York. "You won't have that problem in Moscow," he promised.

I had told the court that it was difficult to criticize Arabs for attacking Americans in the Middle East when Americans were attacking so many Arabs in the United States. Furthermore, the JDL has targeted not only Americans and Arabs, but also Russians, some Israelis, and the diplomatic establishments of twenty countries considered friends and allies of the United States. And I explained that the JDL had gained a reputation worldwide for being intolerant of other religions: They had desecrated and attacked mosques and Christian churches, massacred Muslim worshipers, and attempted to blow up the Dome of the Rock in Jerusalem, the third holiest shrine in Islam.

The JDL had not liked my testimony.

As might be expected, Shadia's worried father made several phone calls to our command center requesting daily updates on the status of his daughter's safety. I did not share confidential source information or any operational details with The Minister, but did give him my honest assessment: "There is no such thing as 100-percent security but I am absolutely confident this team will keep your daughter safe."

My confidence was largely based on the professionalism of the State Department protection team. Each agent was exceptionally well-trained, extremely motivated, and battle tested. Four of the agents were Vietnam veterans with impressive combat records, and the rest had all served in high-risk law enforcement positions before coming to the Department of State. The entire team had worked protective assignments in the United States and several foreign countries. I knew that they all were capable of an aggressive and undiplomatic response should the situation call for it.

It was imperative that the team be informed of all JDL terrorist activities so that we could study their tactics and methods of operation and, if necessary, adjust our own strategies. One of the most important rules in the protection business is to "know your enemy"—learn as much as possible about the group targeting your principal. I taught Shadia's team everything I could about the JDL.

More than a dozen Jewish extremist groups operate in the United States, including the Jewish Armed Resistance, Thunder of Zion, Kahane Chai (Kahane Lives), the Kach Underground Movement, and the Jewish Direct Action, and most are closely linked to or synonymous with the JDL. American Rabbi Meir Kahane founded the JDL in 1968, ostensibly to defend Jews against anti-Semitism. In reality, the JDL emerged out of the racial tensions engendered by the 1968 New York City teachers' strike, which pitted the predominately Jewish teachers' union against militant blacks seeking greater control over their neighborhood schools. Much of the world regarded Rabbi Kahane as a racist and, in 1990, an assassin killed him in New York.

Most Jews and Jewish organizations condemn the JDL, which has committed more acts of terrorism in the United States than Palestinians, Libyans, and Iraqis.

Like most terrorist groups, the JDL arrogantly demands that all Americans think and behave as they dictate—or pay the consequences. Unhappy that the Lebanese-owned Tripoli Restaurant in Manhattan was catering to Arabs, for example, the JDL set it ablaze with a firebomb, killing an elderly woman. When Pan Am agreed to serve as a cargo agent for the luggage of the Soviet airline Aeroflot, the JDL bombed two Pan Am vehicles at Kennedy International Airport. And when Rabbi Kahane announced his opposition to the Camp David Peace Accords, the JDL firebombed eleven Egyptian diplomatic targets in Maryland, Virginia, and New York.

I told my team that the JDL uses many of the tactics that Middle Eastern terrorists were then using, such as simultaneous attacks, mail bombs, booby traps, and double bombs. In one case, the JDL detonated a bomb inside Amtorg, the Soviet trade center in New York, causing extensive damage to the nineteenth floor of the building. As investigators culled through the debris, they discovered a second bomb only a few feet from New York's chief of detectives and other officials. The bomb squad dismantled it just minutes before it was timed to detonate. A JDL member later reported that Rabbi Kahane knew police were investigating the first bomb and purposefully did not warn them about the second device.

I warned the team that the JDL often used diversions to distract security personnel and described the techniques the group would likely use to lure us into a trap. While Secretary of State George Schultz was addressing the United Jewish Appeal in New York, one JDL member staged a loud commotion while a second militant stormed the stage to assault Schultz. Special Agent Gary Gibson broke a thumb wrestling the assailant to the floor.

I informed the team that three JDL members with histories of violence were on Shadia's campus—a professor and two students. I had good reason to believe that the professor had been involved in the threats to Shadia, but we had insufficient evidence to prosecute him.

We shared information about previous attacks on college campuses. I described an incident in which a Jewish militant had climbed to the roof of a building at Hunter College in New York with a sniper rifle and attempted to assassinate a Soviet diplomat. The terrorist missed him but almost hit the diplomat's child. Another agent on Shadia's team, who had just returned from a grueling three-month assignment in Italy, told us that the Jewish Armed Resistance of the JDL had claimed responsibility for killing a Lebanese medical student in Rome.

One agent wanted to know whether any terrorist groups had committed campus crimes that other groups might emulate. Fearing the "copycat" phenomenon, we always reviewed seemingly analogous situations.

I briefed the team on four relevant incidents committed on campuses by several different terrorist groups, including a bombing at the University of Maryland in College Park on June 27, 1981. As five scholars from the People's Republic of China returned to their homes after a campus party, a powerful bomb killed Cho Ren Wu and wounded the other four graduate students. We noted that the terrorists had concealed the bomb inside an outdoor air conditioner similar to the unit attached to Shadia's apartment building. We rigged hers with a wireless portable alarm system and notified the medical school that we would be questioning any "maintenance personnel" seen working on the unit.

The team was concerned that Shadia's unknown enemies might use a mail bomb, a tactic the JDL had often employed both here and in Europe, and contacted Special Agent Bill Penn, the Firearms and Explosive Ordnance Disposal (EOD) Instructor at the U.S. Department of State, who advised us on methods for inspecting and handling Shadia's mail. Bill Penn, my shooting and EOD mentor, had retired from the U.S. Marine Corps and was recognized worldwide as the best of the best in his field. He reminded us that the JDL was strongly suspected of sending a package bomb that had killed a secretary in California.

On July 17, 1980, a U.S. Postal Service worker delivered a package to the offices of ProWest Computer Corporation in Manhattan Beach. The addressee was company owner Brenda Crouthamel. Inside the package was a metal box with an electric cord and typed instructions that read, "I have sent you a prototype of my new invention. . . . Just plug it in and a prerecorded tape will tell you its many functions."

At 4:23 P.M., shortly after Crouthamel had left the building, a thirty-two-year-old secretary and mother of two named Patricia Wilkerson plugged the electric cord into a wall outlet, triggering a blast that killed her and decimated the ProWest offices.

Although some analysts suspected the JDL's involvement, the case languished for eight years before it finally went to trial in 1988. A fingerprint expert testified that prints found beneath the tape on the bomb package belonged to Robert Steven Manning, a known JDL activist with a long history of criminal activity who had moved to Israel. The expert also said that prints on the accompanying letter belonged to Manning's wife, Rochelle.

Born in 1952, Manning grew up in Los Angeles, dropped out of Fairfax High School at age seventeen, and joined the U.S. Army a year later. The army discharged him after only ten months because of his emotional problems and his inability to adjust to military life. In 1972, Manning placed a powerful bomb in the Hollywood home of a Palestinian named Mohammed Shaalh. No one was injured. As with many other JDL attacks, the authorities never recorded the incident as "terrorism." That same year Manning allegedly called a producer of a television sitcom about a Jewish man married to a Catholic woman called *Bridget Loves Bernie* and threatened to kill the producer if he didn't take the show off the air. The JDL did not approve of the intermarriage theme.

On February 7, 1994—fourteen years after Patricia Wilkerson was blown to pieces in her office—a judge sentenced Robert Manning to life in prison.

Shadia had been using a communal curbside mailbox, which we considered a security nightmare for several reasons. Terrorists and common criminals frequently steal mail to obtain information about their target. Someone could place a letter bomb inside or rig the mailbox so that it exploded when opened, an oft-used ploy. If Shadia went to the mailbox every day, she would establish a predictable schedule and location that a bomber, a shooter, or a kidnapper could exploit. Obscured by bushes and trees, the metal mailbox was supposedly securely locked but I easily opened it with a screwdriver.

"Now that you mention it, I am missing two letters from my father," Shadia explained after hearing our briefing. Her father had sent her a letter outlining plans for a family get-together over the Christmas holidays, which apparently "got lost in the mail." If the letter had been stolen, rather than lost, Shadia's pursuers would now know when her apartment would be empty, where and when her flight departed and arrived, the location of the family vacation, and other pertinent operational intelligence. At the team's behest, the family made some changes to their Christmas plans.

We arranged for Shadia's mail to be inspected and picked up at a local post office.

The team studied every past and present JDL action that might provide a clue or a symbolic gesture that would help us protect Shadia. On August 16, 1985, a bomb allegedly planted by the JDL at a building housing the Boston offices of the American-Arab Anti-Discrimination Committee (ADC) blew up in the faces of two bomb disposal experts. Just as Officer Randolph G. LaMattina, forty, placed the bomb into a special trailer used to transport explosives, the device went off, causing extensive damage to both of the officer's hands. The force of the blast injured his fifty-seven-year-old partner, Michael A. Boccuzzi, who was hospitalized overnight with chest pains.

The Arab ADC, patterned after the Jewish Anti-Defamation League, tries to combat stereotypes and misconceptions about Arabs and Muslims by educating Americans, especially the American press. The JDL has delivered numerous threats to the ADC, including one telegram that read: "We have Bassam Shaka's legs," referring to the West Bank mayor who lost both of his legs in 1980 when Jewish terrorists planted a bomb in his car.

One of the greatest challenges facing the ADC is combatting false charges of terrorism, a common tactic of Arab enemies. Terrorists commit a violent act, sometimes against their own organization or people, and then blame the incident on their enemy.

Only hours before Shimon Peres, the former prime minister of Israel, was to speak at the Jacksonville, Florida, Jewish Center on February 13, 1997, police received a 911 call warning that a bomb had been placed in the synagogue. The caller identified himself as a member of "the American Friends of Islamic Jihad."

Police, special agents, and bomb-sniffing dogs searched the synagogue but they did not locate the device.

Nine days after the speech, children who were attending a luncheon after a bat mitzvah found the bomb, picked it up, and began playing with it. The children were trying to tear the tape and a watch off the bomb's casing when two horrified adults noticed their "toy" and rushed it outside.

But Muslim extremists had not planted the bomb. The alleged culprit was Harry Shapiro, thirty-one, an Orthodox Jew and former kosher butcher.

Peres, seventy-four, who won the Nobel Peace Prize in 1994, has long been unpopular with right-wing Jews for his role in opening negotiations with the Palestinians and Arab states.

Shadia's protection team looked at two other bombing incidents that bore striking similarities. Tscherim Soobzokov, an American citizen who had been a member of the Nazi Waffen SS during World War II, was awakened by a neighbor at his Paterson, New Jersey, home at 4:30 A.M. on August 15, 1985. The neighbor told him that his car was on fire. Rushing outside, the sixty-one-year-old Soobzokov tripped a wire that detonated a pipe bomb, killing him and wounding the innocent neighbor. Soobzokov had been accused of falsifying his wartime activities in order to enter this country in 1955, but when he proved to the court that he had disclosed his Waffen SS membership, all charges were dropped. He had worked for the Central Intelligence Agency in the Middle East for many years before moving to America.

Three weeks after the JDL bomb in Boston injured two police officers and the pipe bomb in Paterson killed Soobzokov, another device detonated at 4:40 A.M., this time in Brentwood, New York. The September 6, 1985, explosion of a pipe bomb on the front steps of Elmars Sprogis's home slightly injured the sixty-nine-year-old former Latvian policeman. Sprogis, then a retired construction worker, had recently been cleared on charges that he helped kill Jews during World War II. The terrorist had set a fire to lure Sprogis onto his porch, but an innocent bystander named Robert Seifried saw the blaze first. As he tried to put out the fire, the bomb detonated, blowing off the legs of the young rock and roll drummer. Twenty minutes after the bombing, *Newsday* received a call from the JDL claiming responsibility for the attack.

Once again we had an American attacked on American soil by American terrorists.

The details of the Soobzokov and Sprogis bombings soon became relevant to our protection team when we spotted a large but contained fire inside a metal dumpster next to Shadia's apartment.

Suspecting that the fire might be a terrorist tactic, we moved our protectee to the room farthest away from the fire and called the fire department, warning them not to approach the blaze until we had checked the area for bombs and booby traps. As two agents exited the side and back doorways and searched for a possible ambush team, another agent gingerly approached the dumpster looking for trip wires and booby traps. Noticing a neighbor running toward the dumpster with a fire extinguisher, the agent checking for bombs ordered her away from the fire. Visibly miffed, the woman reluctantly backed away from the fire but not before yelling a few choice obscenities at the agent. "Maybe we should have sacrificed her," the agent joked.

We allowed the contained blaze to burn itself out, rather than risk the lives of the firemen. Although we didn't discover any bombs or snipers, the fire department determined that the blaze was "definitely deliberately set." Was this a terrorist ruse to test our response or to lure us into a trap? Was it a coincidence that a blaze was deliberately set next to Shadia's apartment at 4:30 A.M., the same time of day as the Soobzokov and Sprogis bombings?

Yet another bombing by the JDL, this time at the Santa Ana, California, offices of the ADC had us concerned. The October 11, 1985, blast killed Alex M. Odeh, the West Coast director of the ADC and injured seven other people in nearby offices. The gentle and peaceful forty-one-year-old poet, college professor, father of three little girls, and devout Catholic was a nationalized American citizen of Palestinian descent.

The night before he died, Odeh said in a television interview that it was time for the Americans to "understand the Palestinian side of the story." Odeh offended many people by arguing that Yasser Arafat, the chairman of the Palestine Liberation Organization, was "a man of peace." In the taped interview, Odeh also strongly condemned terrorism and the hijacking of the *Achille Lauro,* but that segment was not broadcast.

It was a beautiful, smog-free Friday morning when Odeh approached the door of his second-floor office. As Odeh unlocked his office and stepped inside, a trip wire attached to the door set off a bomb that tore through the lower half of his body. The explosion showered the palm-lined street below with pieces of furniture, glass, and concrete, and injured seven people—pedestrians and workers in adjoining offices. A timer on the bomb had given the terrorists exactly one minute to set the device and shut the door behind them.

The bomb was similar to the devices that were used against Soobzokov and Sprogis.

One technical aspect of the Odeh assassination particularly worried us: The terrorists who murdered Odeh had first gained entry through a locked room. Campus security had changed Shadia's locks and we had stationed a twenty-four-hour guard inside and outside her on-campus apartment, but we still had to secure the classrooms, Shadia's library study cubicle, and various restrooms. Once, when I was on the campus of the American University Beirut (AUB), a female student discovered a bomb in a locked restroom. Had the student turned the knob on the toilet stall, the device would have detonated.

On Tuesday, May 21, 1991, Professor Ioan Culianu, a forty-one-year-old Romanian native, was found dead inside a locked bathroom stall at the University of Chicago's School of Divinity, directly across the street from Frank Lloyd Wright's famous Robie House. A single bullet wound to the head killed him. A week prior to his murder, Culianu told a graduate student that he feared for his life, that he had been threatened for getting into "dangerous territory" politically.

Reviewing a chronicle of terrorist incidents that occurred on college campuses, our protection team learned that at least six incidents had resulted from lost or stolen keys. A group that bombed a college Reserve Officers' Training Corps office stole the office keys from a professor's coat left unattended in a library. A group that destroyed a college research center obtained the keys from a janitor. And a group that had planned to assassinate a foreign dissident obtained a college dormitory passkey from a campus sympathizer—a fellow student living in the same building.

Campus security and the apartment building manager both allegedly had tightly controlled keys to Shadia's apartment for emergency situations. The manager's key was in an unlocked metal box affixed to the wall in the manager's office. At least nine students, employed part-time by the manager, had access. To demonstrate how tightly controlled the keys were, I waited for the front desk clerk to go to the bathroom, walked into the manager's office and "borrowed" Shadia's apartment key. It was never reported missing.

I also learned that the school had hired campus security guards without conducting background investigations. Since I had recently reviewed more than 100 rapes, robberies, and murders committed by campus security guards in the United States, and since I knew nothing about the backgrounds of the guards on this campus, we replaced Shadia's locks one more time and took control of the keys.

We recommended to Shadia that she move to a new location, but she refused, saying her studies were too demanding and she would soon be returning to Europe. "I'm not going to allow the terrorists to waste any more of my time," she protested.

After she completed the anatomy course at the top of her class, the university offered Shadia a slot in the medical school. She politely refused. "My father and I both think I would be safer in London," she confided in me. The entire protection team understood. There is nothing glamorous about having bodyguards around you twenty-four-hours a day. It is a terrible and intrusive disruption of your life that drastically limits your privacy and personal freedom.

Although the medical school made no effort to recruit me as a student, the team did keep The Minister's daughter safe as I had promised, and I inadvertently discovered the one thing on which a majority of Jews and Arabs could agree: The Jewish Defense League is no different from any other group of terrorists who detonate bombs and commit assassinations.

CHAPTER 4

Trespassers Amongst Us

The Holy Warriors

"I'M AFRAID TO LEAVE MY HOME," THE 49-YEAR-old Iranian confided to me—one day before an assassin killed him inside his Bethesda, Maryland, house. Ali Akbar Tabatabai had served as press counselor at the embassy of Iran in Washington, D.C., under Shah Reza Pahlavi, but on November 4, 1979, supporters of the Ayatollah Khomeini seized the U.S. embassy in Teheran and ousted the Shah. Now living in exile, Tabatabai founded the Iran Freedom Foundation, which bravely condemned Khomeini and publicly supported the United States.

He was also one of my trusted, confidential sources.

Ali Tabatabai supplied me with valuable intelligence that our government used to protect foreign dignitaries, U.S. officials, and average American citizens. One critical document he gave me was a call-to-arms, distributed by the Islamic Guerrillas of America (IGA). The two-page operational leaflet advocated strategically planned terrorism on U.S. soil and intelligently targeted assassinations of U.S. officials and Iranian dissidents. It preached that Muslims should not limit themselves to conventional guerilla weapons such as shotguns, handguns, and bombs, and it claimed that Allah had given permission for warfare in the United States. "Any American can be targeted . . . no American is innocent . . . as long as U.S. foreign policies are to the detriment of the Islamic community," the document concluded. It was especially critical of U.S. support for the "so-called State of Israel."

Tabatabai was well aware that his anti-Khomeini stance was risky. On July 18, 1980, pro-Khomeini Iranians posing as journalists made a failed assassination attempt in Paris on his longtime friend Shahpour Bakhtiar, the former Iranian prime minister. Tabatabai knew that the IGA had at least 30 heavily armed, hard-core members operating within the Maryland–Virginia–Washington area in addition to 200 members in other states. And he knew that the IGA was closely allied with many other fundamentalist Islamic organizations whose memberships included Iranians, Palestinians, and Libyans.

Four days after Bakhtiar escaped death, a twenty-nine-year-old African-American member of the IGA donned a U.S. Postal Service (USPS) uniform, complete with pith helmet, and drove a stolen USPS Jeep to 9313 Friars Road, the elegant home of Ali Tabatabai, and rang the doorbell. Tabatabai's thirty-year-old loyal aide peered through the door's peephole and saw what appeared to be a bored-looking postman, leather mail pouch slung over one shoulder, holding two packages, one on top of the other. What the aide could not see was that the postman's hand, concealed inside the bottom package, was wrapped around a .9-millimeter handgun.

"Good morning, sir," the postman greeted the aide. "Special Delivery packages for Ali Tabatabai." The aide glanced at the packages but the significance of neither one being postmarked or having return addresses did not register until hours later. The aide had neither read the action-packed novel *Six Days of the Condor* nor seen Robert Redford portray Malcolm, the book's protagonist, in the 1975 film. In novelist James Grady's story, a postman rings Malcolm's doorbell, says, "Special Delivery, return receipt requested," steps inside the doorway while Malcolm looks for a pen, pulls "a silenced Sten submachine gun from the [leather] pouch," and opens fire. The aide also had no way of knowing that in the years since the movie's release, members of seven terrorist groups, including the Italian Red Brigades, the Irish Republican Army, and the Puerto Rican Armed Forces of National Liberation in the United States, had posed as postmen to rob armored cars, deliver bombs, or assassinate targets.

"Mr. Tabatabai is very busy," the aide explained to the postman. "I'll sign for him."

"Sorry, but the rules state that the recipient must sign."

Irritated with this stickler for rules, the aide reiterated that Tabatabai was indisposed and again said he would sign and take full responsibility.

"Look, I'm just doing my job," the postman blustered. "If Mr. Tabatabai doesn't want to sign, he can come downtown to pick up the packages." As the postman turned to leave, Tabatabai, who had overheard the entire exchange from the kitchen, allowed his curiosity to overrule his security.

"Okay, okay," Tabatabai yelled to his aide. "I'll take care of it."

The postman's bluff had worked.

As Tabatabai leaned forward to sign for the top package, the assassin pulled his weapon from the other one and fired three hollow-pointed bullets into the diplomat's stomach and chest. Tabatabai staggered backwards but somehow remained standing for a few seconds inside the foyer. As the assassin ran to the Jeep, Tabatabai crashed heavily to the floor, bleeding profusely from his jagged wounds, curled into a fetal position and died.

In a media interview in 1996, the assassin said of the shooting: "I could see the dust jumping from his shirt."

Carelessly leaving the three spent cartridges on the front porch, the assassin drove the Jeep two miles and exchanged vehicles. He then fled to the Algerian embassy where sympathizers allowed him to shower and change clothes. A secret network of Iranian and American terrorists helped him elude capture and fly to Geneva, Switzerland, where he presented himself to the Iranian embassy. Within forty-eight hours of Tabatabai's death, his assassin landed in Teheran and was escorted to a meeting with the foreign minister, Sadegh Ghotbzadeh.

Prior to Tabatabai's death, only a handful of intelligence officers at various law enforcement agencies knew or cared anything about the Islamic Guerrillas of America. When we tried to alert our respective agencies about this emerging, dangerous group, they greeted us with yawns and condescension.

"It usually takes an assassination or two to wake up the bureaucrats," Carl Shoffler, a detective with the intelligence division of the Washington, D.C., Metropolitan Police Department (MPD), noted dryly. Shoffler, along with John Barrett and Paul Leeper, were the plainclothes officers who arrested the five men who later became known as the Watergate burglars. Their arrests on June 17, 1972, at 1:52 A.M. set off a chain of events that ultimately led to the resignation of President Richard M. Nixon.

Detective Shoffler introduced me to two detectives in the MPD intelligence unit, euphemistically called the Investigative Services Division. "Bill Cagney and Everett Obenhein know more about the IGA than anyone else in the country," Shoffler told me.

Intelligence gathering and analysis is like putting together a giant jigsaw puzzle: You take seemingly insignificant pieces and, with dogged persistence, fit them into a coherent whole. Sharing pieces of the puzzle, the law enforcement community in Washington learned that Iranian-born Bahram Nahidian, a naturalized U.S. citizen, was sponsoring many anti-U.S. demonstrations and appeared to be one of Ayatollah Khomeini's IGA point men in America. Stating that he was fighting American imperialism and Zionism, Nahidian met with Khomeini when he was exiled in France, associated with known IGA members, and, in his spare time, made a killing peddling Persian rugs to U.S. citizens. Fearing that the Central Intelligence Agency (CIA) controlled the American media, Nahidian used a shortwave radio in the back of his thriving Georgetown rug shop to keep in touch with Iran.

On November 4, 1979—the same day that Islamic militants stormed the U.S. embassy in Iran and took more than fifty diplomats hostage—Nahidian, Daoud Salahuddin, and a group of Iranians traveled from Washington, D.C., to New York, climbed to the top of the Statue of Liberty, and unfurled a banner bearing anti-shah slogans. The group then chained and locked themselves to a railing, threw away the keys, and waited for police to arrest them.

With the pieces of information I garnered from the MPD and from covert and overt sources that included analysts from the CIA, the Federal Bureau of Investigation (FBI), the New York Police Department (NYPD), the Los Angeles Police Department (LAPD), and the Federal Bureau of Prisons, I formed an accurate but disturbing picture of the IGA. Consequently, when the Command Center of the Department of State initially called me, reporting that "an unidentified Iranian male had been shot in Maryland," I immediately deduced it was an IGA hit and that Ali Tabatabai was the victim. And I more or less intuited that the gunman was one of two U.S. citizens, either Cleven Raphael Holt, also known as (a.k.a.) Isa Abdullah Ali, or David Belfield. We quickly eliminated Abdullah as a suspect when we learned he was fighting alongside Afghan muslims against the Soviets at the time of the murder.

Tabatabai's assassin was born in North Carolina on November 10, 1950. His parents named him David Belfield. When he was two, David's parents took him to Bay Shore, New Jersey, where they both found work at a state mental hospital. In 1968, David enrolled at Washington, D.C.'s Howard

University, a private, well respected, and historically African-American institution. (A few months earlier, racist sniper James Earl Ray had killed civil rights leader Martin Luther King in Memphis and lone gunman Sirhan Sirhan had mortally wounded presidential candidate Robert F. Kennedy in Los Angeles.) At Howard, David became a member of the Black Man's Volunteer Army of Liberation. About six months later David formally converted to Islam and changed his name to Daoud Salahuddin.

He began spending more and more time at a mosque where he learned of an obscure Iranian cleric named Ruhollah Khomeini whose denouncements of the United States' support for Shah Reza Pahlavi began having a ground-swelling grassroots appeal. A still-classified source quoted Salahuddin as saying in 1979, "Khomeini will be our salvation." Salahuddin met other African-Americans at the mosque whom Iranian intelligence operatives would eventually recruit into the IGA.

Two violent, political incidents in the nation's capital galvanized Salahuddin's radical beliefs in the 1970s and highlighted the fragmentation of the militant Muslim community. The first involved a house located at 7700 16th Street, N.W., that was owned by legendary Los Angeles Laker Kareem Abdul-Jabbar. In 1973 he donated the house to Hamaas Abdul Khaalis, leader of the Hanafi Muslims. Khaalis had distributed a tract criticizing Elijah Muhammad, leader of the Nation of Islam in Philadelphia, as a "lying deceiver." In retaliation, seven armed members of the Nation of Islam invaded Khaalis's home on January 18, 1973, and massacred two adult women and five children ranging in age from nine days to twenty-two months. At the time of the murders, Khaalis was grocery shopping for his family.

The attack on his good friend Khaalis enraged Salahuddin, who now had one more reason to hate the Nation of Islam and its spokesman, Louis Farrakhan. Salahuddin and many others in the Muslim community believed that Farrakhan ordered the February 21, 1965, hit on Malcolm X. After creating a diversion in the Audubon Ballroom in Harlem to pull Malcolm X's bodyguards out of position, three men stood up and pumped twenty-one bullets into the charismatic leader. His pregnant wife, Betty Shabbazz, and four young daughters watched him die.

On March 9, 1977, Khaalis and twelve heavily armed Hanafi Muslims seeking revenge for the 1973 murders of Khaalis's family simultaneously stormed three Washington, D.C., buildings, including the Islamic Center located on Embassy Row. At the District Building, the Hanafis charged to the fifth floor looking for Mayor Walter E. Washington and herded hostages into D.C. Councilman Sterling Tucker's office. Hearing a loud commotion, Councilman Marion Barry ran into the hallway and was hit in the chest with a shotgun pellet, which lodged inches from his heart. Moments later, a shotgun blast killed WHUR-FM radio's twenty-four-year-old reporter Maurice Williams as he exited an elevator. Bob Pierce, a young legal intern lying on Sterling Tucker's carpet with the other hostages, heard shotgun blasts and automatic weapons firing in the hallway. A bullet sliced through Pierce's wrist and tore into his chest and back, paralyzing him for life.

At B'nai B'rith's offices, where the Hanafis took most of the hostages, the terrorists allegedly stabbed a black man because he had been working with Jews. At the end of the two-day siege, the Hanafi Muslims had killed one man, seriously wounded two, injured dozens, and held 149 innocent people hostage.

Daoud Salahuddin served as chief of security at the Iranian embassy in Washington, D.C., until the United States and Iran severed diplomatic ties in April 1980. He then became chief of security at the Iranian Interest Section of the Algerian embassy. As of 1997, Ali Akbar Tabatabai's assassin, a native-born American, was still living in Iran and was still a member of an Islamic assassination squad.

***

Shortly after Daoud Salahuddin assassinated Tabatabai, my other murder suspect showed up in the United States. Isa Abdullah Ali, a six-foot-three-inch, 200-pound African American, had finished his stint with the Afghan muslims.

Born September 13, 1956, Abdullah grew up with eight brothers and sisters in Washington, D.C. He dropped out of Paul Junior High School at age fourteen, lied about his age, and joined the U.S. Army. By 1973 he had completed his Special Forces training and had earned a Green Beret. Abdullah then served in Vietnam for four months. The army transferred him to South Korea where he concluded his three-year tour.

Soon after, Abdullah converted to Islam, eventually becoming a member of the Shiite sect.

He said goodbye to his family in December 1980 and traveled to Lebanon where he fought for the Hezbollah (Islamic Jihad) and Amal terrorist organizations. His ambition: to die in battle while capturing Jerusalem from the Israelis.

Abdullah and I coexisted off and on in Beirut during the city's most turbulent period. By 1980, the former "Paris of the Middle East" had become a bombed-out city synonymous with danger. It was a time when Lebanon was still one of the most beautiful countries in the world yet one of the most violent and politically complex. On one assignment, my partners, Chris Leibengood and Jim McWhirter, and I counted thirty-four separate terrorist organizations, nearly forty hostile intelligence services, fourteen organized crime syndicates, and representatives from two invading armies—all headquartered in Beirut.

On any given day we had Christians fighting Muslims, Christians fighting Christians, Syrians fighting Christians, Muslims fighting Muslims, Israelis fighting Palestinians, Palestinians fighting Palestinians, Iranians fighting Iraqis, and Armenians fighting Turks.

While on a surveillance mission of hostile sniper positions, another partner, Tony Deibler, and I observed two squabbling Lebanese Army units square off and shell each other.

It was a wild ride.

On another mission, Tony and our good friend Mohammed were watching my back while I watched a Shiite training camp from a position high in the Lebanese mountains. I observed something unusual.

"Werewolf, this is Falcon," I radioed Tony. "Just spotted a very interesting tourist enter the camp," I whispered to Tony. "Meet me at Volcano ASAP." From a half-mile away from my concealed position, Tony and Mohammed were monitoring two men on a motorcycle who had been tailing me for most of the day. "Volcano" was our prearranged meeting place one mile from the U.S. embassy.

"What's the story with the motorcyclists?"

"Don't know, but not to worry," Tony assured me. "Hollywood just shot out their tires." We called Mohammed "Hollywood" because of his good looks and because he learned English from watching American movies. Hollywood had just demonstrated crisis intervention, Lebanese-style.

He was half Lebanese, half Palestinian, and one of the bravest men I ever knew. He despised my Israeli counterparts "because they stole my house and killed my sister," and the Israelis despised him. But this was Lebanon, after all, where hatred was the raison d'etre. Hollywood is credited with saving several American lives at great risk to himself. The Iranian-backed Hezbollah, the Party of God, later captured and tortured Mohammed. They left him for dead in the streets of Beirut. He survived the ordeal only to be killed one year later during an artillery battle.

At "Volcano" I told my partners the "tourist" might be none other than Isa Abdullah Ali. "I know this guy from Washington," I said. "He used to hang out with David Belfield and the IGA crowd."

Abdullah walked into the terrorist training camp toting an American M16 assault rifle and clad in Vietnam-era camouflage fatigues with what appeared to be U.S. Army Ranger and Airborne insignia. His mission: training Amal fighters—including about twenty-five girls ages thirteen to eighteen—in guerrilla warfare. He was also lending himself out as a sniper. Utilizing a 500-millimeter telescopic sight he had mounted on an M16, Abdullah reportedly killed at least five Israelis and wounded four. "We know about the black American sniper," growled a pro-Israeli militiaman. "And we're going to get him."

Considering Abdullah's loathing of Israel and his ties to Iranian and Palestinian groups in the United States, I wondered whether he had been involved in the assassination of an Israeli air attache in the exclusive Maryland enclave, Chevy Chase. I cabled Washington and reminded headquarters that someone had pumped five .38-caliber rounds into former fighter pilot Colonel Yosef Alon on July 1, 1973. Alon and his wife had just returned home after attending a party at the Israeli Embassy. Mrs. Alon stepped out of the car and walked to the front door, but before her husband could join her, an assailant shot him dead. It was 1:00 A.M.

The Voice of Palestine in Cairo announced that Alon's execution was revenge for the assassination in Paris three days earlier of a forty-one-year-old leader of the violent Palestinian group Black September. The Algerian playwright Mohammed Boudia had spent the night with his mistress and left her shortly before noon on June 28, 1973. He walked past several French children playing in the street, unlocked his car door, and got in. He turned on the ignition. A powerful bomb, planted by Israeli agents, exploded instantly beneath the front seat.

As I feared would happen, my cable had bounced from bureaucrat to bureaucrat and somehow disappeared. Back in Washington months later, I dusted off my original warning, approached a high-ranking political appointee, and requested permission to at least determine Abdullah's whereabouts when Alon died.

"I think your suspect would have been too young for such a crime," the appointee reasoned, at first denying my request. I admitted that Abdullah was a long shot for the Alon assassination but to eliminate him because of his youth was foolhardy. After all, this "youth" earned a Green Beret by the time he was seventeen years old. But the appointee replied coolly, "I'll get back to you on that." I knew my request would disappear forever into a bureaucratic black hole.

Colonel Alon's killers are still unknown and still at large. But those mysterious survival tools that have served me so well, my instincts, tell me that the assassins could well be American citizens.

About five weeks after spotting Abdullah entering the Shiite training camp, I ran into him again at Beirut's famous Commodore Hotel bar, a demilitarized watering hole for diplomats, journalists, spies, gunrunners, drug traffickers, and mercenaries. The Commodore once had a parrot named Coco that could whistle the French national anthem and imitate rifle fire—which almost got him shot on at least four occasions. Abdullah and I greeted each other in Arabic. I sat at one end of the bar sipping a beer, my left foot resting on the bar stool's upper rung so my ankle-holstered .357 magnum was easily accessible. Since this was Beirut, I also carried a .45 automatic in a shoulder holster. Abdullah moved to the opposite end, mingled with some journalists, and remained standing, drinking a Pepsi. Most Muslims don't drink alcohol, at least not in public, and Beirut had banned Coca-Cola because Israel sells it.

I sensed Abdullah found me vaguely familiar, but my new beard, long hair, and dark, desert tan fooled many people into believing I was either an Arab or a Hispanic.

As with so many of the "enemies" I encountered in Vietnam, Colombia, Peru, El Salvador, Russia, and elsewhere, I found Abdullah to be a bright and likable guy. Mentally reviewing Abdullah's background, I had to admit that I admired his warrior spirit: an inner-city kid from White America courageously joins the army at the age of fourteen and, while still a teenager, ships out alone for Afghanistan and Lebanon to fight for his religious faith. Politics aside, the man had spunk.

Sometimes I fear it's all just a silly game. We choose up sides, pledge allegiance to our team, and play our hearts out. All too often, in Africa, Asia, and South America, I sympathized more with the "terrorists" I was assigned to guard against than with the oppressive governments that they were fighting. Time and again I have encountered my enemy and respected him more than the politicians who brought us together.

As I observed Abdullah at the hotel bar with another Hezbollah member and another man I knew to be a mercenary, I felt more confident than ever that he would someday pose a serious threat to American lives, interests, and security. I couldn't help but wonder whether two Americans, both Vietnam veterans from the same hometown, our nation's capital, would end up combatting each other in the streets of Beirut. It seemed almost surreal.

"We need to be more aggressive with this guy," I communicated to headquarters from Beirut. Headquarters reminded me that my primary mission in Beirut was to protect the U.S. ambassador, and not to fight unless I was fired upon. I was ordered to adopt a passive wait-and-see stance concerning Abdullah. An analyst in Washington, I later found out, who had neither been to Beirut nor met Abdullah, had concluded that he was merely a mentally disturbed crackpot whom we shouldn't take seriously.

Those of us in the field were taken aback.

Abdullah was a member of Hezbollah, an American member at that—a dangerous combination. He had once impersonated a U.S. Secret Service agent and still retained identification under his Christian name, Cleven Holt. He would therefore be an ideal choice for collecting intelligence and infiltrating U.S. diplomatic and military interests in Lebanon. He was familiar with military procedures and jargon, had access to U.S. military uniforms, and would have no problem mingling with the American community. And if Abdullah were just "a crackpot," that would have increased, not diminished, his threat.

Under orders, we did not pursue Abdullah, and he left Lebanon on October 5, 1981. He received additional training, practiced his religion, and soldiered with other Islamic militants in Iran. Eight months later, Abdullah returned to Beirut and offered his services to the Palestine Liberation Organization (PLO).

Two years after the armchair analyst delivered his assessment in Washington, the anti-American, Iranian-sponsored Hezbollah, a.k.a. Party of God and Islamic Jihad, bombed the U.S. embassy in Beirut. Six months later, on October 23, 1983, a suicide terrorist drove a bomb-laden truck into the U.S. Marine barracks in Beirut, killing 241 U.S. military personnel. In the aftermath of both bombings, 290 people had died and 200 more had been wounded. During the 1980s, the Hezbollah kidnapped nineteen American diplomats, educators, businessmen, clergy, journalists, and military personnel and assassinated at least four.

Hezbollah gunmen in Beirut briefly kidnapped Tod Robertson, a correspondent for Reuters news service, in 1984. The orchestrator of the kidnapping was none other than Isa Abdullah Ali. Robertson had been asking too many questions about him.

And then in 1986, Abdullah's ambition to be martyred in battle almost came to fruition. Two disguised gunmen, hoping to neutralize the threat posed by Abdullah, ambushed him on a Beirut street. His companions dragged the badly wounded terrorist to cover and then Hezbollah operatives evacuated him to safety. The two mysterious gunmen, one shooter and one back-up, retreated in different directions and disappeared.

Abdullah's mother, brothers, and sisters convinced a reluctant State Department to help return him to the United States for medical treatment.

After recuperating from his wounds but now limping and moving stiffly, Abdullah got a job as a janitor and groundskeeper at Howard University. Many people believed that Abdullah's age and war wounds would end his militant adventures. I was not convinced. Abdullah had braved Vietnam, Afghanistan, Lebanon, and Iran. His religious and political beliefs were, I believe, genuine. Such a man would never be satisfied with cutting grass or cleaning toilets. He was too restless and he would still have that gnawing sense of something unfulfilled. Unlike his brothers and sisters—one is a lawyer, one is a doctor, and another an accountant—Abdullah knows only soldiering. He is a true believer, a warrior at heart, a friend of the PLO, and, more important, a valuable asset to the worldwide Islamic revolution. I felt certain that the Islamic underground would once again recruit his services.

In 1995 I thought it might be interesting to sit down with Abdullah, share stories about Lebanon, Iran, Vietnam, and Afghanistan, and perhaps learn something about his religion and philosophy. But when I tried to locate him in Washington, he had mysteriously disappeared.

On January 24, 1996, an intelligence alert went out warning U.S. and North Atlantic Treaty Organization (NATO) troops enforcing the peace accord in Bosnia-Herzegovina that Abdullah was in the country. A poster with his photograph was circulated at NATO camps. Sources reported that Abdullah was fighting with Islamic fundamentalists who were supporting ethnic Muslims in the bloody Bosnian war. The alert warned that Isa Abdullah Ali (a.k.a. Cleven Holt), an American citizen, should be considered a threat to U.S. and NATO troops.

CHAPTER

5

Deception in Disguise

Terrorist Techniques

PALESTINIAN LEILA KHALED, A WELL-KNOWN FEMALE fighter, once posed as a Spanish tourist, smuggled hand grenades inside the cups of her brassiere, hijacked airplanes for the Popular Front for the Liberation of Palestine (PFLP), and blithely noted, "On some missions girls are better than men . . . We believe that women are more cold blooded." In the society of terrorists, a bomb or a gun is the great sexual equalizer.

Underestimating the female terrorist is one of our most serious security mistakes. Women now make up more than 30 percent of the international terrorist community and vigorously participate in every aspect of guerrilla warfare including surveillance, suicide attacks, and leadership and support roles. They have proven adept at gaining entry into secure areas, luring victims into ambushes, and smuggling and concealing weapons. Female guerrillas have hidden weapons, bombs, and explosives in Tampax and lipstick containers, beneath wigs, inside hollowed-out high heels, and inside cosmetic cases with false bottoms. Three female hijackers wore girdles made of high explosives, and fourteen women are known to have smuggled bombs or automatic weapons in baby carriages.

Female terrorists are powerful weapons of deception.

Women have utilized a device dubbed the large, bowl-shaped "baby bomb," which the terrorist wears beneath her dress, making her look nine months pregnant. The "pregnant" operative then waddles smilingly past security and delivers her "baby" in a restroom or some other strategic location. Before leaving, the female terrorist blows into a thin hose hidden beneath her blouse and inflates a balloon similar in size to a soccer ball. The bomber then exits past security as pregnant as when she entered.

A female Puerto Rican terrorist who bombed a company in New York concealed an explosive device in her baby's diaper.

Female terrorists in the United States have delivered bombs to the U.S. Department of State, the U.S. Capitol, Mobil Oil, and several other targets. More than 110 women have participated in assassinations, bombings, hijackings, and other terrorist activities in the United States alone.

"We learned to use weapons, sex, and flattery for the revolution," a captured twenty-seven-year-old terrorist told her interrogators. Strikingly beautiful and promiscuously violent, the Middle Eastern terrorist had once received training in the Lebanese camp where American-born freelance sniper Isa Abdullah Ali instructed Amal fighters—the Iranian-backed, Shiite paramilitary terrorist group.

Records show that terrorist and guerrilla groups use some form of deception in 90 percent of their operations: disguises or diversions, ploys or props, false stories or false identifications. For example, Kristina Berster, a member of Germany's violent, anti-American Red Army Faction, entered the United States using a fake Iranian passport.

Recognize the deception and we can defeat the enemy.

An effective ruse used by the anti-Castro group, Omega-7, involved a map and a beautiful woman wearing a short, tight dress and a look of befuddlement. The woman stood in front of the Aeroflot airline ticket office in Manhattan where one lone New York Police Department (NYPD) officer stood guard at a fixed post. (The Jewish Defense League had also targeted Aeroflot.) While unfolding the map, the beautiful woman asked the officer for directions, and while he was walking her partway down the block, a second Omega-7 operative placed a bomb and ran. The officer gave chase, the device exploded, and an Omega-7 lookout reportedly fired at the officer from across the street. Fortunately, he missed. Security personnel too often overlook the lookout who stands at a bus stop or sits on a park bench or talks on a pay telephone or acts naturally in innumerable, circumspect scenarios, ready to back up the primary operative or blindside officers when necessary.

"When a woman is involved in an assassination, bombing, or hijacking, the chances of operational success are dramatically increased," a leader of a Palestinian group confessed to me. Middle Eastern extremists have long recognized the importance of female fighters.

In 1975, two would-be assassins, both female—and both American citizens—attempted to kill President Gerald R. Ford in separate incidents. As the chief executive walked from the Senator Hotel to the State Capitol Building in Sacramento, a pretty, long-haired, fawnlike young woman, wearing crimson monkish robes, pulled a .45-caliber automatic from her ankle holster and pointed it at him. A Secret Service agent grabbed the weapon and wrestled the would-be assassin to the ground. Lynette "Squeaky" Fromme was a follower of convicted mass-murderer Charles Manson. At one point before the assassination attempt, in what was then Manson-vogue, she shaved her head and gouged an "X" into her forehead to show her support for the incarcerated leader. Manson instructed his "girls" to play up to older men, and Squeaky was no exception. She had obtained the automatic from a partially blind septuagenarian.

Sara Jane Moore got off one round at President Ford in September 1975 before security personnel subdued and arrested her.

Male terrorists have used the feminine mystique to another deceptive advantage. I know of fourteen separate incidents, including two in the United States, in which male terrorists dressed in drag to commit assassinations, deliver bombs, rob banks, or escape capture. In most of the cases, the terrorists were eventually incarcerated or killed. Mir Aimal Kansi, who shot five people outside of the Central Intelligence Agency's headquarters in Virginia, reportedly disguised himself as a woman, and evaded two traps that State Department and Federal Bureau of Investigation (FBI) agents set for him in his native Pakistan.

Yehiya Ayash, a member of the Issadin Kassam Brigade, the armed wing of Hamas, was the mastermind behind a series of bombings in Israel that killed scores of Israelis and wounded hundreds. Known as "The Engineer," Ayash pioneered the manufacture of explosive suicide belts and recruited young fanatics to detonate the bombs aboard Israeli buses. Palestinians admired him for his ability to avoid capture—he was notorious for slipping through Israeli dragnets dressed as a woman.

On January 5, 1996, in the self-ruled Gaza Strip, The Engineer's luck ran out. An Israeli intelligence team had sneaked into Ayash's home and booby-trapped his portable telephone. The team then dialed The Engineer's number. Just after Ayash answered and the team was certain of his identity, an Israeli operative pressed a button. The booby-trapped portable telephone blew up next to Ayash's ear, killing him instantly.

Other disguises successfully used by terrorists are far less elaborate than dressing in drag. A member of the Justice Commandos of the Armenian Genocide donned a sweatsuit on May 4, 1982, and started running along the streets of Somerville, Massachusetts. As he jogged past the car of honorary Turkish consul Orhan Gunduz, the runner pulled a .9-millimeter automatic from his pants, fired thirteen rounds at point-blank range, and killed Gunduz. The operative reconcealed his weapon and jogged away from the scene, which was but a block from the Somerville police station. Although Gunduz was undoubtedly aware that Armenian terrorists had gunned down dozens of other Turkish diplomats, he probably had conceived a different image of what an assassin looked like.

A similar case occurred just nine days after American-citizen-turned-pro-Khomeini-assassin David Belfield assassinated Ali Akbar Tabatabai in Maryland on July 22, 1980. A black man dressed in a jogging suit ran to the residence of Cambyse Shah-Rais, the head of an anti-Khomeini group called the Movement for the Independence of Iran, known by its Farsi initials, GAMA. A nineteen-year-old Iranian student was sitting in a car outside Shah-Rais's home. Shah-Rais was almost certainly the intended target, but the jogger fired five shots at the student, wounding him once in the stomach. Four days later, on August 3, 1980, Iranian television aired a tape of Shah-Rais making an anti-Khomeini speech in front of the White House. "The forces of Islam who love Khomeini have assassinated Shah-Rais and three other traitors in California," the state-run station broadcast. Iranian television could always be counted on to exaggerate.

Terrorists operating within U.S. borders are increasingly using the "runner ruse" tactic to surveil, attack, and escape unnoticed. A would-be target is not suspicious of the jogger who passes by each morning as he opens his garage door. After a shooting, witnesses hardly notice a man in a sweat suit sprinting down the sidewalk.

In a briefing to the Washington-area law enforcement community in 1983, I was asked to predict twenty-five tactics and deceptive techniques terrorists would utilize in the United States during the next decade. I answered that we would definitely see mass-casualty vehicle bombings by both domestic and foreign groups; terrorists would attempt attacks on several targets simultaneously; terrorists would increasingly impersonate law enforcement personnel; and foreign terrorist groups would increasingly recruit Americans to perform their assassinations and bombings. By 1993, all twenty-five predictions had come true. One of my assertions was that taxis and taxicab drivers would play pivotal roles in future terrorist activities in the United States.

Members of the Islamic Guerillas of America (IGA) and six other terrorist groups landed jobs as taxi drivers during the 1980s. This concerned everyone in law enforcement because cabdrivers had legitimate access to the Department of State, the Blair House, major hotels, and airports, which would bring the operatives too close to foreign dignitaries whom State Department agents and the U.S. Secret Service were protecting. One cab driver can blend in with hundreds of others.

In a large city, no one would be suspicious of a cab parked outside of an embassy, a government building, a private residence. In a large city, just about everyone is anonymous.

Driving a cab provides an ideal cover for the average terrorist to learn the streets of a targeted city and to surveil and gain access to human targets. Both legal and illegal immigrants have found work as easily as they've obtained hackers licenses without background checks. Furthermore, an unlicensed illegal alien driving an unregistered taxi, or "gypsy" cab, doesn't leave a paper trail and is almost invisible to the "system."

The taxi terrorist can work night or day and can vanish for several hours or several months without being missed. Abdelghani Fadil, who was convicted of plotting to blow up several sites in New York, made only $200 a week as a taxi driver but somehow financed several mysterious trips to Egypt, Sudan, South America, and the Netherlands. Like too many other terrorists, Fadil easily gained U.S. citizenship by marrying an American woman with whom he resided just long enough to satisfy the Immigration and Naturalization Service.

By the early 1980s, a number of anti-U.S. groups in the Middle East, who all had operatives in North America, began a particularly devious tactic involving cab drivers.

Typically, the terrorist places his heavy suitcases in the taxi's trunk and then gives the driver an airport, hotel, government building, or other targeted location as his destination. Once there, the passenger leaves his luggage in the trunk and asks the cabbie to keep the meter running while he runs inside to do a quick errand. The terrorist hurries through the front entrance of the targeted location, and as he scurries out a back exit, the explosives in his luggage detonate, killing the hapless driver and anyone else in the vicinity.

My Lebanese partner, Mahmoud, and I witnessed this tactic firsthand while conducting a security advance at an apartment complex in Beirut where the American ambassador would later attend a secret meeting. We felt the shock waves of an explosion two blocks from us and cautiously approached the blast site where a mangled taxi still in flames and the grotesque bottom half of a human being lay amid the smouldering debris. We assumed the body was what remained of the driver. Mahmoud casually kicked what looked like a left-handed glove, discarded near the driver-side door, but we quickly realized it was the taxi driver's hand, jaggedly severed at the wrist.

We did not find any other casualties, and, fearful that the terrorists had planted a second bomb to kill police and rescue workers—a common practice—Mahmoud and I quickly left the carnage and returned to our partially armored all-terrain "battle wagon."

The taxi driver had been duped into delivering the bomb in a failed attempt to assassinate the resident of a private home.

My friend Mahmoud was among fifty-seven Americans and Lebanese killed on April 18, 1983, when an Islamic Jihad suicide bomber drove his explosives-laden vehicle into the

U.S. embassy in Beirut. Special Agent Alan Bigler, my partner and friend, lost most of his face in the blast but survived.

Several of the Islamic extremists who bombed the World Trade Center drove taxis or used taxis in a variety of ways. After the bombers were convicted, a number of media and law enforcement groups asked my company to provide a list of terrorist threats and actual incidents involving taxicabs. I maintain and update threats-to-do-harm files in my database because they can give analysts an insight into the terrorists' methodology and can help predict future terrorist tactics.

Among the eighty incidents my computer, affectionately known as Michelle, printed out were the following:

July 22, 1980.   Musa Abdul Majid, a Washington cabdriver, fraudulently purchased weapons for the IGA and is believed to have supplied the handgun used in the Tabatabai assassination. FBI agents seized eighty boxes of ammunition and numerous weapons from his home. Majid, an American citizen formerly known as Derrick Pritchett, fled the country shortly after the assassination of the anti-Khomeini leader.

January 17, 1986.   Police in Arlington County, Virginia, received information from a confidential source that Libyan operatives had been paid to place bombs in taxicabs serving Washington's National Airport.

April 15, 1986.   A man with a foreign accent called a government agency and warned that explosives would be placed in five taxis that would be parked in strategic locations around the White House.

November 8, 1990.   The FBI arrested Jamal Mohamed Warrayat, a New Jersey taxi driver, for plotting to assassinate President George Bush, Secretary of State James Baker, and members of Congress, and for conspiring to attack military installations in North Carolina, Texas, and Kansas. In a recorded conversation with an undercover officer, Warrayat said in Arabic that he headed a group of seven individuals who were seeking explosives and planning terrorist attacks. Warrayat, a Palestinian, had served four years in the U.S. Army and is reported to have many relatives in Iraq.

February 26, 1993. At least three of the Muslim fundamentalists who were involved in the World Trade Center bombing—Mahmud Abouhalima, Ramzi Ahmed Yousef, and Abdul Rahman Yasin—all drove taxis in New York City.

March 1, 1994. Rashid Baz, a twenty-eight-year-old Lebanese cabdriver opened fire on a van ferrying fifteen Jewish students across the Brooklyn Bridge. One student died; two were seriously wounded. Baz, who fought in the Lebanese civil war, wanted to kill Jews in the United States because an American-born Jewish settler, Baruch Goldstein, had murdered thirty Arabs in a West Bank mosque. Police discovered a cache of weapons in Baz's home, including rifles, shotguns, and handguns, as well as silencers, a bullet-resistant vest, and a stun gun.

October 1, 1995. Sheik Omar Abdul Rahman and nine other Muslim fundamentalists were convicted of conspiring to assassinate political leaders and to bomb the United Nations, the Lincoln and Holland tunnels, the George Washington Bridge, and other targets in New York. At least five of the convicted terrorists drove taxis for a living.

February 28, 1996. Cabdriver Mohammad Ali, thirty-three, an illegal alien from Pakistan, pleaded guilty to charges of threatening the life of Mayor Rudolph Giuliani. Ali had approached Giuliani in Manhattan on November 29, 1995, and threatened to kill him because the mayor had snubbed Palestinian leader Yasser Arafat by ordering him removed from a concert at Lincoln Center. The court sentenced Ali to time served and immigration authorities deported him.

November 2, 1996. Ibrahim Suleiman, thirty-two, a San Antonio, Texas, cab driver was indicted for allegedly lying to a New York federal grand jury about his relationship and travels with terrorists convicted of the World Trade Center bombing. Suleiman, a naturalized U.S. citizen from Kuwait, was also being investigated for immigration and passport fraud.

Sometimes the terrorists are bested by their best-laid plans. On November 5, 1990, Rabbi Meir Kahane, the controversial founder of the Jewish Defense League in the United States and head of the anti-Arab Kach Party in Israel, was speaking to a group of supporters at the Marriott East Side Hotel in Manhattan when a gunman shot and killed him. The assailant ran from the hotel and hopped into a taxi, commandeering it at gunpoint. When the taxi stopped at a red light, the alleged gunman, naturalized American citizen El Sayyid A. Nosair, fled and ran into the path of a uniformed U.S. Postal Service Officer, sixty-five-year-old Carlos Acosta. They exchanged gunfire. Acosta was wounded in the arm and Nosair was hit in the stomach and captured.

It is possible and very probable that the assassination went as planned until the gunman jumped into the wrong taxi. In all likelihood, cabdriver Mahmud Abouhalima (later convicted of the World Trade Center bombing) was waiting outside the Marriott in his taxi, the intended getaway car. The problem was that most New York cabs look alike.

* * *

Like baseball pitchers who alternately throw curve balls, sliders, and fast balls to confuse batters, terrorists routinely change their means of concealing weapons and delivering bombs to confuse law enforcement officials. Squeaky Fromme and other assassins have hidden guns in ankle holsters. Others have used folded newspapers, bags of groceries, a coat draped over an arm, the inside of an umbrella, a vendor's cart. One assailant, dressed in tennis whites, pulled a submachine gun from a racquet case. Sometimes terrorists deliver explosive devices "by hand" on suicide belts, under maternity clothes, inside briefcases. Sometimes they plant booby traps. And sometimes they send the bomb through the U.S. mail. Letter bombs travel the same way other first-class mail is transported—by truck, by rail, and aboard commercial airliners —putting postal workers, airline passengers, and other innocent bystanders at risk.

Operatives of the Puerto Rican Armed Resistance mailed a bomb to the U.S. ambassador to the United Nations Jeanne Kirkpatrick at the U.S. Mission. A mailroom clerk dumped the suspicious-looking package onto the desk of my Diplomatic Security Service partner Dave Haas. The parcel weighed eight ounces, measured seven inches long, and had no return address. As Haas surgically removed a small piece of brown wrapping paper, he exposed red and blue wires protruding from a Head & Shoulders dandruff shampoo box. Agent Haas perceptively reasoned that wires in a shampoo box had a singular purpose and called the NYPD bomb squad. They found a metal pipe tightly packed with explosives concealed inside the small box. "Your partner would have been horribly maimed or killed if he had opened the package," a bomb-squad member told me. The terrorists had not only booby-trapped the parcel, they had also set a timing device as backup.

In 1973, an IRA letter bomb exploded at the British embassy in Washington, seriously maiming a secretary named Nora Murray. During 1997, the *Al Hayat* newspaper office at the National Press Building in Washington, D.C., received two letter bombs disguised as musical Christmas cards and postmarked Alexandria, Egypt. Three others arrived at the federal prison in Leavenworth, Kansas.

Cuban terrorists living in the United States vary their tactics of terror, and their disruptive methods seem so easy in the final analysis. Omega-7 detonated three bombs on March 25, 1979—one at New York's Kennedy International Airport and the others in New Jersey. The Kennedy Airport bomb exploded inside a suitcase that was being loaded onto a U.S. passenger aircraft. Had it detonated ten minutes later, the bomb would have blown up when the plane was airborne. The incident signaled that Omega-7 was willing to sacrifice innocent lives and risk massive casualties to make their point.

Omega-7 often utilized clever diversionary tactics to pull security away from their posts. On October 27, 1979, two police officers left their stations at the Cuban Mission to the United Nations to remove a disorderly and seemingly intoxicated man. As they escorted him to the front of the building, an Omega-7 member placed a bomb at the side entrance. The bomb brought down a wall, and the "drunk" member of the terrorist team set a new sidewalk record for the 100-yard dash.

Political assassins create illusions with the aid of props to deceive the public and security personnel. In one instance, an assassin wearing a cast on his arm inside a sling registered at a small Middle Eastern hotel and signed in under an alias. We could not pull a handwriting sample or fingerprints because the assassin had asked the front desk clerk to fill out the form. "I'll dictate," he told the clerk.

The sling concealed the .9-millimeter handgun the assassin used to kill a rival militia member as the victim exited an elevator into the hotel lobby.

The "athletic-looking man" with an arm in a cast and a sling appeared harmless and nonthreatening to security personnel and distracted potential witnesses. The people we interviewed all agreed that the assailant had a bad arm, but almost everyone described the man differently, including one female sympathizer who was intentionally misleading us.

Police and others searched in vain and found a discarded sling and cast in an airport restroom the next day. After the fact, the front desk clerk told us, "I thought it was odd that the guest paid in cash and didn't have any luggage . . . The way he paced around the elevator, I knew he was stalking someone."

Between 1980 and 1997, 648 members of domestic and international terrorist organizations have hidden in plain sight on campuses of higher education, either employed by or attending classes at American colleges and universities. These deceivers have attempted or committed at least 309 acts of political violence.

At the University of California at Riverside on May 29, 1994, a gunman broke through a crowd and wounded controversial former Nation of Islam spokesman Khallid Abdul Muhammad and three of his bodyguards. Muhammad had just given a speech on campus and was leaving a heavily guarded auditorium at the time.

Officials at the University of South Florida knew very little about a professor who taught Middle Eastern studies until Fathi Shakaki, a leader of the Islamic Jihad, was assassinated in Malta in 1995. The professor quit his university post, moved to the Middle East, and allegedly became a new leader of the terrorist group. Islamic Jihad, or Hezbollah as it is commonly called, is one of the most violent anti-American groups in the world.

On August 5, 1985, in Chicago, five members of the Puerto Rican Armed Forces of National Liberation (FALN) were convicted of conspiring to plant bombs at several military installations. Three of the five terrorists were either employed by or enrolled at the University of Illinois Medical Center, Northeastern Illinois University, or the University of Illinois at Chicago.

In Philadelphia, FBI undercover agents arrested two Libyan intelligence officers who were enrolled at the University of Pennsylvania and the University of Maryland. Both men were convicted and sentenced to jail for buying handguns and silencers for paid assassins. Libyan terrorists have also been enrolled at Georgetown University, Texas Tech University, and seven other schools in the United States.

Four Iranian students enrolled at Mankato State University in Minnesota conspired to kidnap Governor Al Quie during a reception for foreign students at the governor's mansion in St. Paul. Police caught the students in the act and jailed them on charges of conspiracy to commit kidnapping, conspiracy to commit assault, and possession of illegal firearms.

Five Iranians attempting to smuggle high-powered rifles, sniper scopes, and ammunition onto a New York-bound plane from Washington–Baltimore International Airport were arrested. Among the students' possessions the police also discovered a map of Washington, D.C., with certain embassies marked and circled. All five Iranians attended schools in Maryland.

In September 1997, President Bill Clinton and his wife Hillary escorted their teen-aged daughter, Chelsea, to Stanford University in California. Every effort is being made to ensure that the First Daughter's four years in college will be a normal experience. Chelsea is one of many high-threat college students who will require protection by the Secret Service, the Department of State, and other government and private agencies. The agents assigned to these protection teams face one of the most demanding and challenging assignments of their careers.

CHAPTER

6

Viva la Resistance

Puerto Rican Nationalist Extremists

NOVEMBER 1, 1950, WAS AN UNSEASONABLY HOT 85 degrees in Washington, D.C. Two well-dressed men checked out of the Harris Hotel at 17 Massachusetts Avenue that day, hailed a taxi, and asked to be driven to Blair House, across the street from 1600 Pennsylvania Avenue. President Harry S. Truman had temporarily taken up residence at the mansion while the White House underwent reconstruction.

At 2:15 P.M., the two men hopped out of the taxi and hurriedly separated, passing by the painted wooden guard houses that flanked Blair House. Each man had his right hand buried in a jacket pocket. As they made their way from opposite directions to within ten paces of the residence's stairway, twenty-one-year-old Oscar Collazo drew a German Walther P-38 automatic from his pocket, aimed it at the back of White House guard Private Donald Birdzell, and fired. The weapon jammed. Recognizing the distinctive "click," Private Birdzell wheeled around just as the man unjammed his gun. Collazo then unloaded eight rounds at Birdzell, hitting the uniformed private once in the right leg. The assailant released the spent magazine from his P-38 and quickly slipped in a fresh ten-round magazine.

As Birdzell hobbled into the street and bravely drew fire away from Truman's transient home, Collazo unloaded several more rounds; one shattered Birdzell's right patella. Bleeding profusely, Birdzell fell to his knees near the streetcar tracks, drew his .38-caliber revolver, and returned fire.

By now, bullets flew from all directions.

Armed with a German Luger, 25-year-old Griselio Torresola moved to the westernmost wooden guard house and mortally wounded Private Leslie Coffelt, point blank, in the chest and abdomen. He quickly turned and then hit White House policeman Joseph Downs three times.

Torresola fought his way over a small hedge and onto a plot of grass where he fired off several rounds, hitting Birdzell in his good leg. Before collapsing face forward onto the streetcar tracks, Birdzell once again returned fire. Private Joseph Davidson and lone Secret Service agent Floyd Boring opened up on Collazo, and a single round from Boring's gun hit Collazo in the chest, putting him out of action.

As he lay dying in his guardhouse, Private Coffelt managed to stop Torresola with a single bullet to the head.

Awakened from a nap by the shooting, President Truman, still in his underwear, rushed to an open window and saw pedestrians scattering and police officers swarming to the scene. A guard ordered him away from the window. The president obeyed.

Stray bullets whizzed in all directions; one round strafed an Officer Preston of the Metropolitan Police Department, slicing through his jacket. When the gunfire first erupted, he was directing traffic on Pennsylvania Avenue. By the time Preston rushed into the fray, weapon drawn, the fighting was over. Still wearing a hat, the wounded Collazo was stretched out at the foot of the Blair House steps, his fashionable gray suit splattered with red. Torresola lay crumpled next to a hedge, dead.

Investigators learned that Collazo and Torresola were Puerto Rican nationalists from New York who sought independence for the island. They had holed up in the Harris Hotel for two days while they worked out the final details of their plan to shoot their way into Blair House and assassinate the president of the United States.

Secret Service agents found two letters on Torresola's body from Harvard-educated Pedro Albizu Campos, leader of the extremist Puerto Rican Nationalist Party. Asserting that the United States had no legal claim to Puerto Rico, Campos had long called for Puerto Ricans to take action against the "American oppressors."

Had the gunmen read the morning newspapers, they would have known the papers always published the president's daily schedule. They would have known that on November 1, President Truman was scheduled to attend a ceremony honoring the late Sir John Dill, Britain's wartime chief of staff, at Arlington National Cemetery. Had they waited another thirty minutes, President Truman would have walked down the ten granite steps of Blair House in plain view.

Ironically, President Truman was a strong advocate of Puerto Rican independence.

By 1950, assassins had shot and killed three American presidents: Lincoln, Garfield, and McKinley. Armed attackers had tried to kill President Theodore Roosevelt and president-elect Franklin D. Roosevelt. But the attack on President Truman was the first time assassins tried to shoot their way into a U.S. president's home; it was the first time more than one assailant participated in an attack; and it was the first time the assailants belonged to a domestic terrorist organization.

For the next four years, the Puerto Rican Nationalist Party and other Puerto Rican extremist groups plotted to overthrow the American government and participated in a number of low-level bombings and shootings, mostly in Puerto Rico. But the group would not get the front-page publicity they sought until March 1, 1954.

On the floor of the House of Representatives that day, a member had demanded a quorum count. House Speaker Joe Martin announced that 243 members were present. At 2:32 P.M., four members of the Puerto Rican Nationalist Party, three men and one woman, stood up in the spectators' gallery, screamed "Viva Puerto Rico" and began shooting German Lugers and other handguns at members of Congress.

Some House members initially thought the loud popping sounds were firecrackers. Others who saw the guns thought the ammunition were blanks. Someone even yelled, "Those shots are just in play."

"The hell they are," shouted Representative George S. Long, a Democrat from Louisiana whose brother Huey was murdered outside the Louisiana state Senate chamber in Baton Rouge. "Those are real."

House members fell and dived for cover as bullets ricocheted off walls and ripped through furniture. Everyone quickly realized what was really happening.

Holding the large Luger in her small hands, Lolita Lebron, the petite and fiery leader of the gang, unloaded her magazine at the members of Congress, then threw down her handgun. She pulled out a Puerto Rican flag, began waving it wildly and screamed, "Viva Puerto Rico!" while her male comrades blasted the House floor.

A rapid staccato of thirty-one rounds rained down indiscriminately. A bullet hit Representative Alvin Bentley in the chest just below the heart, tearing through his liver and other vital organs. Representative Ben Jensen was standing near the door when a bullet slammed into his shoulder. Jensen staggered to the members' cloakroom and collapsed. Through clenched teeth he implored another member, "Did they get me in the spine?" In an odd twist, Jensen had proposed placing a glass partition in front of the galleries to protect members of Congress. Later at the hospital he noted, "I sure bet they'll listen to me now."

Representatives George Fallon, Clifford Davis, and Kenneth Roberts all suffered leg wounds.

The assault lasted fewer than three minutes. Previously disabled by surprise and fear, the House members and stunned visitors quickly recovered and reacted, rushing toward the visitors' gallery as the Puerto Rican terrorists, smoking guns still in hand, madly pushed their way out to escape. One terrorist reloaded his weapon as he ran, but when he tried to fire, the automatic jammed.

Lolita Lebron, still clutching her flag, ran out first and was quickly collared and subdued by three unidentified men. A visitor named Frank Wise helped three other men tackle a male comrade trailing behind Lebron and wrestle him to the floor. Wise was recuperating from an illness and had come to Capitol Hill for the relaxation that his doctor had prescribed. Boyd Crawford, a 190-pound clerk of the House Foreign Affairs Committee, thrust his fingers under the trigger guard of the assailant's Luger, preventing him from shooting.

Another spectator jumped the second male terrorist and held him in a headlock, but the terrorist still had a grip on his gun. The doorman, William Belcher, and seventy-one-year-old Capitol policeman A. S. (Buck) Rodgers jumped in to help. Rodgers, who had been a Texas farmer before becoming a policeman, karate-chopped the gunman's wrist. The heavy Luger clattered to the floor. Belcher later suffered a heart attack and was hospitalized.

The third terrorist escaped the angry crowd but police later arrested him at the bus station.

On the House floor, representatives A. L. Miller of Nebraska and Walter H. Judd of Minnesota, both medical doctors, administered to the five wounded congressmen.

The attack was the most serious incident to occur at the U.S. Capitol since the British burned it in 1814.

* * *

Christopher Columbus landed on the island of Puerto Rico on November 14, 1493. Spaniards took over the island in 1508 and introduced slavery in 1518, which was not abolished there until 1873.

After the United States won the Spanish-American War, Spain ceded the island to America in 1898. American troops landed in the southern bay of Guanica on July 25, 1898.

The Commonwealth of Puerto Rico is a self-governing territory of the United States; its residents become U.S. citizens at birth but they cannot vote in U.S. presidential and congressional elections. The United States provides the 3.8 million islanders with considerable economic assistance and they are not required to pay federal taxes.

The proindependence movement, now consisting of a dozen different groups, continues fighting what it deems is the U.S. occupation of Puerto Rico.

By the 1970s, five known Puerto Rican independence groups operated in the United States but only one advocated violence and operated covertly: the Fuerzas Armadas de Liberacion Nacional Puertoriquena (FALN), or Armed Forces of National Liberation. FALN superseded the more widely known Puerto Rican terrorist group, the Armed Revolutionary Independence Movement whose Spanish initials spell MIRA.

The armed assaults on Blair House and the U.S. House of Representatives gave proindependence groups a new cause celebre: the release of the Puerto Rican prisoners convicted of those crimes. Their tactics to press their demands were always violent and sometimes symbolic.

George Washington delivered his farewell address to the officers who had served under him during the Revolutionary War at New York's Fraunces Tavern on December 4, 1783. Almost 200 years later, two men strolled into the historic colonnaded, yellow-brick structure on Broad and Pearl Streets at 1:10 P.M. and had no difficulty disappearing into the lunchtime crowd, many of whom were Wall Street executives. Like many other diners, one of the men carried a black attache case. But this briefcase was different: It contained a propane tank and explosives equivalent to ten sticks of dynamite. The men departed the restaurant a few minutes after setting the briefcase against a wall. They started running.

The incredibly powerful blast at 1:20 P.M., on that cold January 24, 1975, day turned silverware and china into lethal shrapnel. The explosion forcibly hurled diners from their tables into a confusion of screams and flying debris. A fork blew through one man's heart and killed him. Another diner was decapitated. Shards of glass ripped into Edythe Brous, a secretary who had been celebrating her birthday with her boss.

As dozens of police cars, ambulances, and fire trucks converged on the scene, they saw bleeding diners stumbling into the street and people collapsed on the sidewalk, groaning in pain. Diners still inside the restaurant were suffering from fractured limbs and ribs, severe cuts, burns, and other injuries. Some people, blinded and deafened by the blast, groped in the darkness, looking for an exit.

The final tally: four people dead and fifty-six people injured, some horribly.

Claiming responsibility for the bombing, the FALN demanded the unconditional release of five nationalists imprisoned on the mainland for the 1950 and 1954 attacks.

To this day, the FALN is among the groups seeking complete independence for the island from the United States. The vast majority of Puerto Ricans, however, advocate either the retention of the present commonwealth status or statehood, following the example of Alaska and Hawaii. Only a tiny percentage of voters in Puerto Rico relish independence. Over the past decade, the police and Federal Bureau of Investigation (FBI) agents have confiscated 296 sticks of dynamite and 350 pounds of incendiary materials from various FALN safe houses. As impressive as these numbers may seem, they are dwarfed by the lethal supplies Puerto Rican terrorists have stolen and stockpiled.

Between the 1950 attempted assassination of President Truman and 1998, Puerto Rican extremists conspired to assassinate President Dwight D. Eisenhower, Secretary of State John Foster Dulles, and FBI Director J. Edgar Hoover, and they have committed more than 500 acts of terrorism in the United States and Puerto Rico. In 1981 police discovered a powerful car bomb at a convention center in Puerto Rico where Secretary of State Henry Kissinger was to deliver a speech.

They also maimed a twenty-two-year-old New York City Police Department (NYPD) officer named Angel Poggi.

Officer Poggi was on his first night of patrol in Harlem on December 11, 1974, when Puerto Rican terrorists lured him to a tenement building with a bogus report of a dead body. As Poggi pushed open a door leading to the supposed victim, he triggered a booby-trap that exploded in his face. The blast badly disfigured Officer Poggi and cost him his right eye.

Angel Poggi became the seventh law enforcement officer to be wounded or killed by Puerto Rican extremists.

Very few terrorist groups in the world have hit such a wide range of targets as the Puerto Rican terrorists. The FALN planted a bomb inside an umbrella stand at a Mobil Oil office in New York that killed one man and wounded seven. Two pipe bombs exploded in a locker at New York's Penn Station on December 21, 1980, forcing thousands of holiday travelers into the streets. An FALN bomb exploded on March 17, 1981, injuring two New York police officers. And when devices exploded on New Year's Eve in 1982, they badly maimed three policemen: one NYPD officer had his leg amputated, one lost fingers, and the third lost an eye and his hearing. On May 16, 1981, a booby-trapped briefcase that the FALN left in a restroom at JFK International Airport killed an innocent man.

Fortunately, two other bombs, one in a congested terminal area and another in a women's restroom, were discovered and defused.

To commemorate the anniversary of the attack on the U.S. House of Representatives, the FALN detonated bombs at four Wall Street targets in 1982. The FALN has bombed fifty-one banks, department stores, and government targets.

Although many of the terrorists are dedicated and determined "soldiers," the individual FALN operatives are neither a Superman nor a James Bond—none of us is—so they are not invincible. After assembling scores of bombs for the FALN over the years, William Morales finally made a mistake. On a hot summer night in Queens, New York, Morales was building a pipe bomb in his apartment when something went terribly wrong. As he connected a wristwatch—a favorite FALN timing mechanism—the bomb exploded, blasting off his lower jaw, lips, and both hands. Police arrived eighteen minutes later and found Morales standing over the toilet. Despite horrific pain and shock, the bomb-maker was trying to tear up his address book and other evidence with his teeth. (In the Marine Corps we called such disciplined, stoic behavior "hard Corps.") Police found enough explosives in his apartment to build more than 2,000 bombs.

Convicted of numerous bombing offenses and sentenced to ninety-nine years in prison, Morales was allowed to recuperate before serving time. He requested a transfer to New York City's Bellevue Hospital so therapists could teach him how to use the stumps that once had been his hands.

Morales proved a fast learner.

The tough-spirited terrorist obtained a pair of bolt-cutters, tied them to his stumps, and worked a hole in a wire-enclosed, fourth-floor window. Morales shinnied down a rope made from sheets, thirty feet to the ground where FALN allies from the Black Liberation Army waited, armed and prepared to fight off any pursuers.

The FALN will remain well supplied with firearms and bombs from robbing gun stores and armories, and from burglarizing construction sites that use explosives. Some of their operations have been brazen, well-planned, and, for the public, very scary.

On January 14, 1980, the FALN raided the National Guard Armory in Wisconsin, hoping to steal antitank rockets, mortars, M-60 machine guns, and M-16 automatic shoulder weapons. FALN operatives studied the inside of the armory by filling out applications for the National Guard. While inside they asked relevant questions, were given a tour of the complex, and shown where the weapons were stored.

The operatives watching the outside perimeter determined who worked at the armory, what vehicles the workers drove, the shifts, and the busy and slow times. They took many pictures.

Two days before the attack, group members arrived from three different states and met at a house in Milwaukee. The members wore masks and gloves at the house as disguises and to keep the house fingerprint-free in case the FBI had the house under surveillance. The masks also served another purpose: to protect their identities from each other in case of a mole (a double agent) in the group or if a member got caught and made a plea-bargain agreement.

The terrorists then deposited a number of stolen escape vehicles, mostly vans, at three different locations. (The FALN used vans in 90 percent of their operations.) They planned to escape in three different directions to confuse police and reduce the chances that the entire team would be captured.

On the morning of the attack, two armed terrorists entered the armory when it first opened. Three women immediately followed as lookouts. All five terrorists wore U.S. Army fatigues. A sixth terrorist cut the base telephone lines, and other operatives manned the three escape vehicles.

The terrorists ordered the armory personnel to unlock the vault where the rockets, mortars, and machine guns were stored but none of the employees had the keys or the combination. Satisfied that the frightened employees were telling the truth, the terrorists stole base personnel files and a couple of handguns, and drove away. Each of the three teams ditched its escape van and then jumped into three different vehicles. The terrorists then returned to their homes in other states practically empty-handed but a bit wiser. They would not make the same mistakes in the future.

Another violent, proindependence group, possibly more brazen than its brother-in-arms, is the Macheteros. They first made headlines on August 24, 1978, when they murdered San Juan policeman Julio Rodriguez Rivera for his uniform and marked patrol car. But they gained worldwide infamy in 1979, when two of their vehicles boxed in a ponderous U.S. Navy bus, carrying nineteen enlisted personnel, as it crept along a Puerto Rican highway. From the back of a pickup truck, the Macheteros sprayed the bus with stolen M-16 automatic rifles, killing two servicemen and wounding ten.

This dangerous band shot a military policeman at Fort Buchanan in 1981, wounding the MP in his shoulder. Machetero members driving a Cadillac sprayed bullets at four sailors assigned to the USS *Pensacola* as the men walked back to their ship. In that 1981 ambush, one sailor died; the other three suffered serious wounds.

They are a cold, clever, and dangerous group. A dozen Macheteros, dressed in U.S. Army and law enforcement uniforms, attacked an armored bank truck in Puerto Rico on July 15, 1983, killed the driver, and stole more than $500,000. In another incident, Macheteros wearing police uniforms opened fire on an armored bank vehicle. When the real police arrived, they were fooled by the imposters. The fake police suddenly opened fire on the real police, killing a bystander before fleeing.

On October 30, 1983, the Macheteros fired a stolen light anti-tank weapon (LAW) at the Federal Building in Hato Rey, Puerto Rico. The terrorists were aiming at the FBI offices but hit offices of the U.S. Department of Agriculture instead. In 1985 they fired a rocket at a U.S. courthouse in Puerto Rico.

But it was a single, well-planned and well-executed assault that underscored the sophisticated operational capabilities of the Macheteros and illustrated the embarrassing inadequacy of our own security.

Shortly after midnight on January 12, 1981, eleven male and female members of the Marxist–Leninist group cut a hole in an eight-foot-high chain-link fence and sneaked onto the tarmac of Puerto Rico's Muniz Air National Guard Base. The invaders planted twenty-six pipe bombs in thirteen U.S. military jet fighters. The operation took fewer than nine minutes, and, at the time, it was the most costly terrorist attack against a U.S. military installation in history.

The day after the attack, I arrived to investigate the crime. The carcasses of eight A-7D Corsair II jet fighters still smouldered; two others suffered less damage but were still intact. The blasts also destroyed a retired, engineless F-104 Starfire formerly used as a display, and raked rescue equipment parked near the aircraft. Three bombs did not detonate and a Navy bomb squad removed them from two extant planes. Near the wreckage the Macheteros left their calling card: a machete.

Fortunately, the bombs destroyed and incapacitated only machines, but the sad scene reminded me of the worst battlefields I had seen in Vietnam and Beirut.

Only two security officers guarded the forty-five-acre Muniz Air National Guard Base, which is situated between swampland and the San Juan International Airport. One guard had a fixed post at the base entrance; the other patrolled the base perimeter. The inadequate lighting outside the perimeter fence afforded the Macheteros the cover of darkness; they could approach the fence with little fear of being spotted. I surmised that the rebels waited for the guards to change shifts before cutting the hole through the chain links. (Worldwide, dozens of terrorist attacks have occurred during shift change.) During the brief, ten-minute interval when no one was on the tarmac, the raiders strategically placed the bombs.

In this case, a lone guard could not have stopped the attack; terrorist lookouts would probably have killed him. Even if the lone guard could have radioed for help, the response time of the security team would have been too slow. By then, the terrorists would have been long gone.

The date of the attack was a significant anniversary for the Macheteros. January 12 is the anniversary of the birth of Eugenio Maria de Hostos, a nineteenth-century patriot active in the struggle for independence from Spain. Proindependence groups traditionally marked the day with protests against U.S. rule in Puerto Rico. January 12, 1981, also coincided with the convening of the new legislative session.

Published reports indicated that the insurrectionists' bombs caused more than $40 million in damages, but the actual replacement cost for the lost and damaged aircraft was more than $100 million.

Before I flew out of San Juan's International Airport, a senior airport executive told me that the "attack at the National Guard Base could just as easily have occurred right here."

As expensive and humiliating as the bombing of the Muniz National Guard Base was for the United States, a second incident committed in Hartford, Connecticut, gave the Macheteros legendary status in the world terrorist community.

It also made them very rich.

Victor Gerena was born in 1958 and grew up in one of Hartford's poorest public housing projects, the eldest child in a fatherless family of six. Although he never had much money, he somehow stayed out of trouble and showed great promise in high school both academically and athletically: He was captain of the wrestling team, played football, and ran track. Gerena won the respect of many teachers and even interned at the State Capitol. After enrolling in Annhurst College, a conservative Roman Catholic school, he dropped out after only one semester.

Gerena worked at various low-paying, dead-end jobs, including a stint as a security guard, but lost the positions for tardiness or failing to show up.

Then Wells Fargo Guard Services hired him and he suddenly became a polite, punctual, model employee—always neatly dressed in full uniform and always one of the company's hardest workers.

One detail Wells Fargo didn't know about Gerena was his membership in the Macheteros, a group that has robbed more money from armored car companies than any other terrorist group in the world.

Gerena earned $4.75 an hour riding armored cars all over the state of Connecticut. He picked up and delivered mountains of other people's money.

On September 12, 1983, at 9:00 P.M., Gerena's boss, Jim McKeon, was at his desk in the Hartford Wells Fargo office surrounded by millions of dollars in cash. Nearby a driver named Tim Gerard rested his feet and eyes.

When Gerena suddenly grabbed the gun from McKeon's holster and pointed at his boss' head, Gerard jumped to his feet. Gerena pulled back the hammer on his handgun and warned Gerard not to move.

Gerard and McKeon reported that Gerena told them that he was tired of working for other people. He tied up his coworkers and injected both men with a sleep-inducing substance, which didn't work.

Gerena then loaded 1,150 pounds of money—$7,007,150 in cash—into his car and drove away. He currently lives in Cuba.

"Seven million dollars will sure buy a lot of guns and explosives," a Central Intelligence Agency buddy said to me.

Many experts say that we have heard the last of the FALN, the Macheteros, and a dozen other groups fighting for Puerto Rican independence. But they are wrong. The groups went underground after a number of arrests but they will regroup, reorganize, and return. Some time down the line they will hit us harder than ever.

CHAPTER 7

Their War Rages On

Cuban Rebels in Exile

"THE TARGET IS IN SIGHT, THE TARGET IS IN SIGHT!" radioed the pilot of a Cuban MIG-29. Cruising at 500 miles per hour off Havana on February 24, 1996, Lieutenant Colonel Lorenzo Alberto Perez and a Cuban MIG-23 pilot were closing in fast on three unarmed civilian Cessna aircraft flying in international airspace above the Straits of Florida.

The U.S. National Security Agency was recording and transmitting every word the two Cuban airmen said air-to-air and air-to-ground control. American intelligence files on Perez dated back many years. Top-notch Soviet fighter pilots had trained him, and he was a veteran with forty-nine combat missions in Angola.

"I know Perez's voice, his fighting tactics. I studied his weaknesses. He's good, but, God, I'd love to take him on," a graduate of America's Top Gun fighter pilot program told me. "If I got any closer to him, I'd be sleeping with his wife."

"If presented with an option, choose his mistress. She's gorgeous," I advised.

A Cuban ground controller asked Perez, "What's the color and type of aircraft?"

"It's a Cessna 337," answered the colonel. "I have it in lock-on! I have it in lock-on!" he shouted.

"We have it in lock-on," the MIG-23 pilot echoed. "Give us authorization to destroy."

The pilots had locked their missile-guidance systems onto one of three Cessnas piloted by members of the Miami-based Cuban Brothers to the Rescue, a Cuban-American anti-Castro group. Founded by Jose Basulto, the group had rescued hundreds of refugees who had fled Cuba on rafts and small vessels. On January 13, 1996, Brothers to the Rescue dropped leaflets over Havana, urging Cubans to overthrow Castro. They were on a return mission.

"Authorized to destroy," Cuban ground control ordered. Confirming that he had correctly understood, Colonel Perez replied, "I'm going to fire at it."

"Authorized to destroy it," ground control repeated.

"First launch," Colonel Perez radioed at precisely 3:21 P.M. One of twelve heat-seeking missiles affixed beneath his high-speed, exceptionally maneuverable MIG-29 dropped away and blasted forward. Seconds later, the nine-foot long, 225-pound missile loaded with fifteen pounds of high explosives in its nose reduced the tiny Cessna to a giant fireball, instantly killing pilots Carlos Costa and Pablo Morales. Pieces of plane and human bodies plummeted to the sea.

"We took out his balls!" exclaimed Colonel Perez to ground control.

"This one won't mess around anymore!" radioed the MIG-23 pilot.

Mario de la Peña and Vietnam veteran Armando Alejandre, Jr., the pilots of the second Cessna, didn't see the explosion but they had seen the MIGs in the area and tried to alert their leader, Jose Basulto.

"There's a MIG in the air, bogie in the air," the pilots warned Basulto.

"I've seen them. They are north of us at this time," Basulto replied. Unaware that the fireball was the remains of his friends, he radioed, "The MIGs dropped a flare, apparently to take reference. . . ."

"Have you heard from Carlos?" the other pilots interrupted.

"Negative," Basulto answered.

By that time, Colonel Perez had spotted Peña and Alejandre's Cessna outside the twelve-mile limit of Cuban airspace but inside the Air Defense Identification Zone, or ADIZ. Civilian aircraft can pass through that buffer zone if they announce and identify themselves. Before the three Brothers to the Rescue planes entered the ADIZ, they made themselves known.

Nevertheless, Colonel Perez signaled Cuban ground control, "Second launch." Seconds later, a second fireball. The captain of a fishing vessel later reported that bits of man and machine splashed all around his boat.

"The second one is destroyed!" Colonel Perez yelled triumphantly. "Motherland or death! Balls! Yeeehaa!"

In the distance, Basulto continued trying to raise his friends on the radio, "Come in Carlos, are you there? Mario, do you copy? Mario, is that you?" No one answered. Believing he had just seen another flare from the Cuban fighters, Basulto keyed his microphone one more time and warned, "I guess we better get out of here. Get back to base."

By then the MIGs were running low on fuel and were ordered back to base. Brigadier General Ruben Martinez Puente ordered another pair of MIGs to take off from the Cuban military air base at San Antonio de Los Banos and give chase. At 600 miles per hour, the MIGs quickly caught up with Basulto's little Cessna, spotting it "maneuvering" through clouds at 6,500 feet.

"Report the registration number," Cuban ground control commanded. The pilots could not.

General Puente realized the two fighter jets were a few minutes from downtown Key West, Florida, and ordered them home. "Abort mission," ground control radioed at 3:52 P.M.

"Copied," answered the lead MIG pilot. "Abort mission."

Upon landing his plane safely at Opa-Locka Airport north of Miami, Basulto learned that his friends Carlos, Mario, Armando, and Pablo were all dead. He burst into tears.

* * *

On April 17, 1961, a 1,453-man army of Cuban exiles whom the Central Intelligence Agency (CIA) had recruited and trained, invaded Cuba at Bahia de Cohinos, the Bay of Pigs. Jose Basulto had fled Cuba in 1959 and was one of the first volunteers in the CIA-backed Brigade 2506. The CIA drilled him in sabotage and intelligence gathering, and in how to be a radio operator. Six weeks before the ill-fated attempt to overthrow Fidel Castro, Basulto was smuggled into Cuba.

Poor intelligence, even poorer planning, and security leaks plagued the invasion from the outset. The strategists arrogantly underestimated both Castro's strength and the combative spirit of his supporters. Military experts had warned them that the attack was foolhardy and unlikely to succeed, but they recklessly charged ahead.

The CIA absurdly selected the swampy Bay of Pigs as the landing site for an amphibious assault, basing their decision on sixty-six-year-old surveys. For the covert operation to work, intelligence gathering was critical, yet the CIA had only twenty-eight agents in Cuba and none was ever able to penetrate the higher echelons of Castro's regime. Ironically, Castro had more agents in the United States at that time than we had in Cuba. Although he didn't know where or when the attack would be, Castro knew it was imminent and had established contingency plans should the enemy land at the Bay of Pigs.

Castro's intelligence agents told him that the CIA was instructing Cuban counterrevolutionaries in military warfare at camps in Florida, Guatemala, and Nicaragua. Furthermore, the press leaked stories about the invasion just weeks before it launched. A January 10, 1961, front-page headline in the *New York Times* blared: "U.S. Helps Train An Anti-Castro Force At Secret Guatemalan Air-Ground Base." The *Times* reporter had had no difficulty sneaking into the camp. Guatemala's *La Hora* and the U.S. political weekly *The Nation* also disclosed details of the military drills.

Castro's 182,000-man army and militia, many of them U.S.-trained, vastly outnumbered the 1,453 rebels whose success was dependent on U.S. air support promised to them by the CIA. The air strikes were to soften the landing site and destroy Castro's tanks and aircraft, and every military expert of merit recognized that without the air support, the rebels had virtually no chance at all.

Disgracefully and inexplicably, President John F. Kennedy canceled the air support shortly before the battle began.

By the third day of fighting, Castro's forces had killed 114 members of Brigade 2506 and captured 1,289. Most of the captured rebels were locked up in Cuban prisons until December 23, 1963, when the United States paid Castro $53 million in food and medicine as ransom for their release. Ramon Conte and other *brigadistas,* however, languished much longer: Conte remained imprisoned for nearly twenty-six years. Only about fifty counterrevolutionaries, including those who had infiltrated the island earlier, either never landed or escaped.

One of the rebels able to elude capture was Jose Basulto, who went to Miami where he joined the CIA-sponsored anti-Castro group Revolutionary Student Directorate. Sixteen months later, operatives in Cuba tipped off Basulto's group that Castro would be at the Hornedo de Rosita Hotel the night of August 24, 1962, drinking with his Soviet advisers. Basulto, Juan

Salvat, and other group members mounted a 20-millimeter Lahti cannon onto a thirty-one foot Bertram and sailed toward Cuba for what would be the first of many terrorist attacks by Cuban exiles. Unlike the Bay of Pigs, this operation was not CIA sponsored. The CIA had not even given its consent. Floating in darkness 200 yards off Havana, Basulto fired 8-inch, armor-piercing rounds into the hotel where frightened guests dived for cover as shells blasted through the hotel walls. No one was injured. Castro had not yet arrived. Basulto and his crew high-tailed it back to Miami, hotly pursued by the Cuban Coast Guard.

Seven months after the hotel assault, Basulto and about fifty other Bay of Pigs veterans enlisted in the U.S. Army where most earned officers' commissions. Basulto was trained in psychological warfare. Following their stints in the U.S. military, Basulto and hundreds of other Cuban exiles became active in the anti-Castro underground.

In 1976, delegates from twenty Cuban exile paramilitary groups secretly met and vowed never to end their armed struggle against Castro until he was dead and their homeland was free. Alpha 66, the Cuban National Liberation Front, Brigade 2506, Accion Cubana, Omega-7, and the Coordination of the United Revolutionary Organization (CORU) were among the groups represented. From January 1976 to January 1996, this loose federation committed nearly 250 acts of terrorism within U.S. borders.

Although the groups regard Cuba as their primary target, they have also drawn a bead on the interests of twenty-nine other countries, including Mexico, Costa Rica, Argentina, Chile, Venezuela, and other Latin American nations. If a country trades with Cuba, then the anti-Castro element considers it fair game for bombings. If a nation incarcerates an operative of one of the terrorist organizations, the extremists bomb that nation's interests. When a president of Panama visited Cuba and kissed Castro, the Cuban exiles retaliated by detonating a powerful bomb in front of the Panamanian embassy in Caracas.

The right-wing extremists have attacked hotels, court-houses, diplomats and diplomatic establishments, private businesses, ships within U.S. territorial waters, and airports and aircraft. Shortly after 1:00 P.M., on October 6, 1976, Cubana Airlines flight 455 lifted off from Seawell Airport in Barbados and began climbing into calm, clear blue skies en route to sunny Jamaica. Nine minutes after takeoff, the Seawell control tower picked up the panicked voice of flight 455's pilot shout-ing, "We have an explosion . . . Descending fast . . . We have fire on board!" Some of the radio transmission was garbled, but the control tower heard a second explosion and then the pilot yelling, "Shut the door! . . . Going down!"

Witnesses on the ground watched in horror as the DC-8 spit and sputtered, spewed forth thick black smoke, tumbled, and then nose-dived into the Caribbean Sea only a few miles from shore. All seventy-three passengers and crew members perished, including the entire sixteen-member Cuban national fencing team, medical students, and Korean and Latin Ameri-can citizens.

The operative had concealed explosives inside of two hollowed-out cameras and had hidden a special "pencil" det-onator inside a tube of Colgate toothpaste. (Depending on the pencil's color, the detonators trigger an explosion in eight or forty-five minutes, or two, eight, or twenty-four hours.) Be-fore the plane landed at Seawell Airport, the terrorist planted the bomb in one of the restrooms. The passengers and crew on that leg of the flight later remembered the suspect as being excessively anxious. When flight 455 stopped in Barbados to refuel, the bomber walked off the plane then took a taxi to Hotel Village. The cab driver recalled that the suspect asked him to stop along the way so he could look up at the sky. He, too, thought the suspect was extremely nervous and agitated.

I don't have independent confirmation, but my sources in Venezuela are convinced that the chief suspect acted independently. The CIA allegedly had trained him in firearms, photography, and the manufacturing of bombs, and the anti-Castro movement reportedly paid him $25,000 for the job. Blame for the bombing was assigned to the Cuban terrorist organization CORU, led by Dr. Orlando Bosch, a U.S.-trained pediatrician.

Bosch and Castro had both attended the University of Havana in the late 1940s where they were friends and where both men served on the student council. The doctor left Cuba in 1952 to serve a two-year internship at Toledo Hospital in Ohio and then returned to Fulgencio Batista y Zaldivar's Cuban dictatorship. Initially Bosch believed in Castro's revolution against Batista but quickly became disillusioned. He led a group of anti-Castro guerillas, but after his squad ran out of supplies and he learned that Castro had sentenced him to death, Bosch and his followers fled to Florida. In 1960, he hooked up with the CIA.

During the 1960s, Bosch participated in several anti-Castro activities in Cuba but soon grew disenchanted with the CIA and the Kennedy administration. He banded together a group of Cuban exiles who eventually committed three-dozen bombings, kidnappings, and assassinations in the United States and Latin America.

Launching an armed expedition against a foreign government from U.S. soil violates the Neutrality Act. Although he was arrested seven times in four years for violating neutrality laws, Bosch always went free, the charges dismissed.

"Bosch was guilty as hell," said a former Justice Department official familiar with the cases but who did not work directly on them. "But if we convicted him, we'd also have to convict the CIA and a lot of other Americans . . . it would be very messy politically."

The CIA began realizing that they had helped create a monster when the Costa Ricans arrested Bosch in 1976 and he confessed that his mission there was to assassinate Secretary of State Henry Kissinger who was scheduled to arrive five days henceforth.

The consummate wheeler-dealer, Bosch usually managed to finagle his way out of hot spots or at least receive reduced sentences by threatening retaliatory terrorism or by offering political favors to South American leaders. On August 13, 1976, a terrorist walked across an unguarded tarmac at Miami International Airport and placed a bomb near a parked Venezuelan Air Force plane. The ensuing explosion caused some damage but no injuries. A caller claiming to represent the Luis Boitel group said the bomb was revenge for the Venezuelan government's detention of CORU's Orlando Bosch.

Following the 1985 Palestinian takeover of the Italian cruise ship *Achille Lauro,* several experts appeared on news programs and described maritime terrorism as "new." Various groups of extremists, however, had bombed, hijacked, rocketed, or fired on 281 maritime vessels between 1968 and 1985. In 1968, Bosch and a *compadre* crouched behind bushes lining the median strip of Miami's MacArthur Causeway. They awaited the Polish ship *Polanica* that they believed was en route to trade with Cuba. The men sprang up, hoisted a bazooka to Bosch's shoulder, fired a rocket at the hull, and caused minor damage to the ship. The Miami police thwarted an earlier attempt by Cuban extremists to blow up a docked ship when they arrested the primary operative as he towed the torpedo through rush-hour traffic.

The 281 maritime vessels attacked by terrorists plus the siege of the *Achille Lauro* did not include criminal acts committed by modern-day pirates or so-called common criminals or vessels attacked by military services. Cuban Action, a.k.a. Cuban Power, detonated five bombs on ships in 1968. Bosch planted a bomb on the *Asaka Maru,* intending an explosion at sea that would kill dozens of Japanese sailors, but it blew while the ship was still anchored in Tampa Bay. The Cuban exiles' bombs also exploded on the Japanese vessel *Mikagesaw Maru* and on two British freighters, the *Caribbean Venture* and the *Lancastrian Prince.*

Following the murder of a Cuban national in the Bahamas in 1973, the Cuban Liberation Front planted two bombs in the hull of the Bahamian ship *Mereghan II,* which was docked on the Miami River. The blasts tore two three-by-two-foot holes in the ship. A year later, three days after Christmas, anti-Castro guerillas hurled a hand grenade onto the *Maxim Gorki,* which was berthed in San Juan. Two Soviet crew members were wounded, one seriously.

In 1979, the Irish Republican Army detonated a remote-controlled bomb on a twenty-nine-foot yacht off the coast of Ireland, killing Lord Mountbatten, his grandson, and two boat hands. A Basque separatist group sank a Spanish Navy patrol boat in 1984, killing one crewman. Between May 1985 and May 1997, terrorists attacked at least 168 maritime vessels. Throughout the 1980s and 1990s, anti-Castro groups kept up assaults on maritime boats and ships, mostly strafing them with automatic fire.

* * *

"We felt totally used and abandoned," fumed a sixty-two-year-old veteran of the Bay of Pigs invasion. I interviewed him and three other active members of Cuban exile groups operating in the United States on the thirty-sixth anniversary of the Bay of Pigs debacle, April 17, 1997. "Without air support, the invasion became a suicide mission. The most powerful nation in the world drew us into the fray and then betrayed us."

"We will attack Castro and his communist government until he is dead and our homeland is returned to democracy," railed a sixty-year-old member of the failed invasion force.

He still trains most weekends in steamy camps in the Florida Everglades.

"I will fight Castro in the United States, Cuba, and anywhere else in the world until Cuba is free," boasted a twenty-seven-year-old refugee who seemed more interested in adventure than politics.

A U.S.-born man in his mid-twenties told me, "Castro killed my father and my half-brother." He had never been to Cuba and spoke only elementary Spanish, but he added, "I'll fight him with bombs and bullets."

For those four men and hundreds of other Cuban Americans, their fight against communism did not end with the Cold War. Their war rages on.

The terror of the February 24, 1996, MIG attack on the Cuban Brothers to the Rescue Cessnas ensures that the violent anti-Castro underground operating inside the United States will thrive as long as Castro is alive. At a news conference the day after the shootings, Madeleine K. Albright, then-U.S. delegate to the United Nations, said the downing of the planes was just plain murder. "This isn't *cojones*," Albright remarked, referring to the MIG pilots' use of Spanish slang for testicles, "This is cowardice."

Appendix: Cuban Chronicle of Terror

Although dozens of anti-Castro Cuban exiles have been incarcerated in the United States and in Cuba for terrorist activities, new recruits keep the movement alive. The following chronicle is a short sampling of the types of incidents Cuban exile groups have been involved in since 1976.

September 21, 1976, Washington, D.C. Orlando Letelier, former Chilean ambassador to the United States, and his American assistant Ronni Moffitt were killed at Sheridan Circle when a bomb exploded beneath the ambassador's car. The Chilean intelligence service hired American Michael Townley to kill Letelier. Townley recruited and trained three Omega-7 members in bomb-making and made them part of the assassination team.

September 7, 1977, Washington, D.C.   The Pedro Luis Boitel Commandos, an anti-Castro Cuban exile group, detonated bombs near the White House fence and at the offices of the then Soviet Union's Aeroflot Airlines and maritime mission.

September 19, 1977, Florida.   The Pedro Luis Boitel Commandos exploded bombs at four hotels in Miami: The Fontainebleau, Eden Roc, Sheraton Four Ambassadors, and Dupont Plaza.

December 23, 1977, Florida.   A bomb exploded in the Miami office of Venezuela's VIASA Airlines. The powerful explosion occurred a few hours after the departure of VIASA's first scheduled flight from Chicago to Cuba since the 1960s.

December 26, 1977, New York.   Omega-7 detonated a bomb in the offices of the Venezuelan consulate in New York.

May 18, 1979, Washington, D.C.   Omega-7 detonated a bomb behind the three-story building that houses the Cuban Interest Section.

October 1979, New York.   The Cuban government reported to U.S. officials that they had uncovered a plot to assassinate Castro when he spoke at the United Nations in New York. The night before Castro's arrival, Federal Bureau of Investigation (FBI) and U.S. Secret Service agents arrested nine anti-Castro Cuban exiles, who had traveled from Miami, at a Manhattan apartment. The men were taken into custody and sent back to Miami, but never charged. (Castro's intelligence agents have successfully infiltrated most of the anti-Castro Cuban exile groups in the United States.)

November 25, 1979, New Jersey. Omega-7 assassinated Jose Negrin in front of his young son in Union City. Negrin advocated talks with Castro. The weapon used to kill him was later used to assassinate Cuban diplomat Felix Garcia in New York.

December 7, 1979, New York. Omega-7 detonated a bomb at the Cuban U.N. Mission, injuring two police officers. The explosion broke windows within a three-block area.

February 1981, Florida. The FBI arrested seven members of Alpha 66 who were planning to travel to Cuba by ship and conduct sabotage and assassinations. The agents recovered one 55-millimeter antitank weapon, one Colt AR-15 semiautomatic rifle, seven handguns, and other weapons.

September 11, 1981, Florida. Omega-7 bombs exploded at the Mexican consulate in Miami and at the *Republica* magazine office, causing extensive damage at both locations.

February 2, 1982, Florida. Omega-7 bombed the *Republica* magazine office.

September 2, 1982, Florida. Omega-7 detonated a bomb in a restroom adjoining the Venezuelan consulate.

September 2, 1982, Illinois. An Omega-7 operative detonated a bomb at a Chicago book store that allegedly sold Communist literature.

January 11, 1983, Florida. An explosion at the Padron Cigar Company was claimed by Omega-7.

May 27, 1983, Florida. Omega-7 detonated a bomb at the Continental National Bank in Miami.

May 2, 1987, Florida. Cuban exile extremists detonated pipe bombs at three businesses that ship clothes and medical supplies to Cuba from South Florida.

October 7, 1992, Cuba. A beach at the Cuban resort Varadero was strafed by machine-gun fire from a boat off shore. Comandos L claimed credit for the attack.

May 20, 1993, Florida. U.S. Customs agents arrested nine members of the Cuban exile group, Alpha 66, after searching their twenty-five-foot boat and discovering seven semiautomatic assault rifles, hand grenades, pipe bombs, a grenade launcher, and handguns. At the time of his arrest, one of the men said they were on their way to attack Cuba and spark a revolution.

September 26, 1993, Florida. Using radio transmissions beamed at Cuba, Alpha 66 encouraged sympathizers to harass and attack foreign tourists visiting Cuba. Alpha 66 wanted to create bad publicity for Cuban tourism, a $500 million a year industry.

March 11, 1994, Cuba. Miami-based Alpha 66 commandos claimed responsibility for strafing the Guitant Cayo Coco Beach Hotel near Camagüey, 300 miles east of Havana.

May 10, 1994, Florida. Rodolfo Frometa, forty-eight, chief of operations for Alpha 66, announced that his group had formed a separate organization called Comandos F-4 that would carry out a "new military strategy" against the Castro government. He said that Comandos F-4 would have the co-operation of dissidents inside Cuba.

September 4, 1994, Florida. Two Molotov cocktails were thrown at the offices of the Spanish-language entertainment magazine *Replica,* whose editor has called for a full dialogue with the Cuban government.

September 29, 1994, Florida. Two members of the anti-Castro group Comandos F-4 were convicted of conspiring to export a Stinger antiaircraft missile, three antitank rockets, and a grenade launcher to Cuba.

October 15, 1994, Cuba.   Seven Cuban-American members of the Party of National Democratic Unity (PUND), a Miami-based commando group, were arrested in Cuba after an exchange of gunfire with security forces. A Cuban fisherman was killed in the gun battle and three of the exiled commandos were injured. One of the commandos, Armando Sosa, fifty-six, had spent seventeen years as a political prisoner in Cuba. "Cuba has to be free, no matter if Armando dies," said Sosa's brother. Like hundreds of anti-Castro Cubans, Sosa believes that bullets, not words, will oust Castro. On April 25, 1996, a Cuban court sentenced one of the raiders, Humberto Real Suarez, twenty-six, to death by firing squad. Sosa and the other five commandos were sentenced to thirty-year prison terms.

November 2, 1994, Florida.   The FBI arrested three Cuban-American men who were planning to set fire to a warehouse used by a group that advocates establishing relations with Cuba. Unaware that the police were watching, the men showed up with ten gallons of gas, fuses, and a fully loaded handgun. The warehouse was used to store twenty tons of medical supplies destined to be donated to the Cuban people by a group that favors lifting the U.S. trade embargo against Cuba. The men were members of the November 30th Movement and the Movement of Revolutionary Recovery.

September 23, 1995, Florida.   The Cuban exile paramilitary group PUND, sponsored a concert to fund weapons purchases and sabotage operations against Castro's government. Staged at the Orange Bowl, the concert consisted of an impressive collection of Cuban stars.

December 16, 1995, California.   The FBI raided the office of a kitchen supply dealer in Los Angeles, charged three men with planning to invade Cuba, and removed two truckloads of military equipment including AK-47 assault rifles, scuba gear, body armor, self-inflating rubber rafts with motors, and radios. The three men, Rene Cruz, sixty-eight, his son, Rene Jr., forty-seven, and an employee, Rafael Garcia, all belonged to an anti-Castro group called Comandos Unidos. Agents discovered invasion plans that called for the men to attack Cuba on December 31, 1995, capture additional weapons after landing in Cuba, and provoke an armed uprising by Cubans in three cities. Investigators also learned that the men had purchased a sixty-foot shrimp boat in Mississippi capable of transporting up to thirty people to Cuba. Cruz Sr. spent seventeen years in prison for his opposition to Castro.

July 11, 1996, Florida. Cuban exiles firebombed the Centro Vasco Restaurant because the owner had announced plans to feature Cuban singer Rosita Fornes on July 28. Fornes lives in Cuba and the exiles accuse her of being pro-Castro.

April 13 to September 4, 1997, Cuba. Ten bombings were reported at hotels in Havana and Veradero. Three bombs exploded at the Copacabana Hotel on September 4, killing one Italian tourist and causing considerable damage. The Cuban government believes that the bombings were part of a campaign by exiles in Florida to damage tourism in Cuba.

CHAPTER 8

Lodging Bullets

Hotels as Terrorist Territory

THE SIXTY-THREE-YEAR-OLD GREEK-AMERICAN WAS among a swarm of demonstrators at New York's Waldorf Astoria Hotel. As the 400 angry Greeks and Cypriots protested outside the hotel on July 26, 1976, Bulent Ecevit, the controversial former Turkish prime minister, was inside addressing an equal number of people attending a Federation of Turkish-American Societies' dinner. Ecevit headed the opposition to the Turkish government and was touring the United States to drum up support and money for his political campaign.

Ecevit had been prime minister when the Turks invaded Northern Cyprus in 1974, an incident that eventually led to the toppling of the Greek government. Special agents from the Diplomatic Security Service (DSS) at the U.S. Department of State were assigned to keep him alive.

As the former prime minister was leaving the hotel, an assassin pushed to the front of the Greek-American's group and pointed a handgun at him. The grey-haired Greek-American remembers seeing Stavros Sykopetritis aim at our State Department protectee. He remembers a woman—a fellow demonstrator—

scream, "Kill him!" And the former member of the Union of Greeks and Cypriots of the United States also remembers seeing agents "from all over the place" fly into the gunman's body. "It looked like when an entire football team tackles a ball carrier," he reported with considerable animation.

"But my most vivid memory of that night," he said, "was when your agents pulled the gunman's arm off."

Ecevit departed the Waldorf's Empire Room dwarfed by six-foot-five-inch, 275-pound Fred Lecker, the Special Agent in Charge (SAIC) on his right. Scanning the crowd and flanking Ecevit's left was six-foot-three-inch, 270-pound George Mitchell, a former Baltimore police officer. At 9:15 P.M., as supporters in the hotel lobby shouted questions and tried to shake Ecevit's hand, Stavros Sykopetritis, standing five feet from the ex-premier, pulled a .25-caliber automatic from his pocket and pointed it at Ecevit's head.

Agent Bernard Johnson spotted it and yelled, "Gun!"

From the raised platform where he had been standing, Johnson leapt over two Ecevit supporters and slammed his body into Sykopetritis. Agents Horace Mitchell, Richard Rowan, and Dave Haas plowed into the gunman from different directions and secured his free hand as Johnson fought for control of the gun. In rapid succession, New York Police Department (NYPD) officer Kevin Walker and Detective John McCormack aggressively flew into the fray.

Still struggling with the gunman, Mitchell grabbed the man's left arm to handcuff him but the man resisted, pulling his arm beneath him. Mitchell grasped the gunman's arm again, and again the man pulled away. With adrenaline coursing through his veins, Mitchell yanked the man's arm using all his might, severing the gunman's arm at the shoulder. Aghast, Mitchell stared wide-eyed at the amputated arm in his hands.

"All I could think about was the police brutality charges," commented one State Department agent.

For several seconds, time stood still. Mitchell's frozen face melted into a smile. Sykopetritis was a member of a Greek-Cypriot terrorist group called EOAK, and a few years earlier he accidentally blew off his arm while making a bomb. Horace Mitchell was holding a prosthesis.

Agents Haas and Johnson instantly dislodged the weapon from the gunman's exceptionally powerful right hand. Sykopetritis had pointed the fully loaded, chambered .25-caliber automatic at Haas's stomach three seconds earlier.

While Horace Mitchell and the others were struggling with Sykopetritis, Agents Fred Lecker and George Mitchell covered Ecevit with their massive bodies. They were hustling him through the hotel to the prearranged escape route when Tony Deibler radioed Lecker that the location had "too many demonstrators." Agent Deibler had parked Ecevit's armored limousine outside the back exit.

Lecker took the most direct route possible to the safe exit —through a ballroom dance competition held in a giant hall. As the music played, Lecker, Mitchell, and five other agents, weapons drawn, swept their protectee across the dance floor among the 500 formally dressed men and women. One male dancer hollered, "What's the meaning of this!" and women screamed, but the competitors moved aside and allowed the burly bunch to pass.

When the team exited the back door to the hotel, Agent Deibler had the armored limousine in place with the lead car and the follow cars manned and in position. They drove Ecevit to another hotel where Agent Jeff Bozworth met the entire entourage curbside and guided the team to a suite of rooms that were already being guarded.

An estimated 100,000 persons gave Ecevit a hero's welcome when he returned to Turkey a week after the attempt on his life. Three camels were slaughtered roadside near the airport in a traditional Muslim sacrifice celebrating his escape.

Ironically, the attempt on Ecevit's life in New York revived his flagging popularity in Turkey.

* * *

Hotels offer terrorists an excellent venue for stalking and assaulting their prey. The most obvious reason is that thousands of controversial politicians, diplomats, executives, and other tempting targets attend hotel functions or stay in hotels as guests each year.

Security at even the best hotels tends to be limited and has rarely challenged or intimidated a serious assassin or terrorist team. Most hotels have numerous entrances, and access controls are either nonexistent or relatively easy to defeat. Furthermore, the chaotic, come-and-go public atmosphere of hotels is particularly conducive to criminal ruse, disguise, and escape. Assassins in the hotel environment have mingled unnoticed with crowds of international visitors or have posed as waiters, security guards, members of the press, and room service personnel. Sometimes the assassins create diversions and sometimes they simply charge into the hotel and start shooting.

Most of the famous assassinations and attempted assassinations in the United States have occurred in the hotel environment. On October 14, 1912, John Schrank shot former President Theodore Roosevelt in the chest from a range of six feet as the candidate was leaving a hotel after attending a dinner there. The gunshot slightly wounded Roosevelt, who was campaigning in Wisconsin for a comeback against his presidential successor, William Howard Taft. Roosevelt delivered a scheduled speech before going to the hospital; John Schrank was sent to an asylum.

In 1968, within a few months of each other, two assassins murdered two prominent Americans at hotels and changed the political landscape of the United States.

Dr. Martin Luther King, the eloquent, thirty-nine-year-old Black Baptist minister, was in Memphis, Tennessee, on

April 4, 1968, supporting striking municipal sanitation workers. He had led the massive civil rights movement since the 1950s by employing nonviolent direct action. Dr. King was standing on the balcony outside room 306 at the Lorraine Hotel when escaped convict James Earl Ray fired a single round from a rifle, hitting the 1964 Nobel Peace Prize winner in the neck. Ray confessed to the assassination on March 10, 1969, and was sentenced to ninety-nine years in prison. In July 1991, the Lorraine Hotel was dedicated as the National Civil Rights Museum in King's honor.

A few months after the King tragedy, Palestinian refugee Sirhan Sirhan murdered Senator Robert F. Kennedy inside the Ambassador Hotel in Los Angeles.

Just after the presidential front-runner finished addressing supporters, Kennedy's security detail escorted him through the hotel's kitchen to avoid the large crowds. Sirhan was hiding behind a food-tray rack in the kitchen service area. As Kennedy moved through the food service section, shaking hands with workers, Sirhan leapt from his hiding place and shouted, "Kennedy, you son of a bitch." The assassin pointed a .22-caliber handgun one inch from Kennedy's head and pulled the trigger. As Kennedy fell to the floor, mortally wounded, Sirhan pumped two more rounds into the listless body. The gunman then fired five more rounds, hitting five bystanders.

Sirhan Sirhan, twenty-four, grew up on the West Bank and viewed Kennedy as a constant collaborator with Israel. He was especially angry that Kennedy proposed the sale of advanced jet fighters to the Jewish state.

On April 24, 1970, two members of the Taiwanese Independence Movement (TIM) attempted to assassinate Chiang Ching-Kuo, a son of nationalist Chinese dictator Chiang Kai-shek, as he arrived at the Plaza Hotel in New York. Bill McFadden, a special agent with the U.S. Department of State, wrestled Cornell University doctoral student Peter Huang

Wen-hsiung to the ground and grabbed his loaded handgun. The assailant's brother-in-law, Cheng Tzu-tsai, charged forward with a knife but was arrested by NYPD officers.

Chiang, then vice premier, was not hurt in the attack and succeeded Chiang Kai-shek as president eight years later.

After pleading guilty at their arraignment, Huang and Cheng jumped bail and fled to Europe. Cheng was extradited to the United States and served a five-year sentence for attempted murder, but Huang remained underground until 1996 when, at the age of fifty-nine, he returned to Taiwan. (Although TIM is not a widely known group, it is still active and has been responsible for dozens of bombings, including one at the Taiwanese Mission in Bethesda, Maryland, and another on China Airlines at Los Angeles International Airport, for assassinations, and for other terrorist activities in the United States.)

A double assassination on January 27, 1973, at the Biltmore Hotel in Santa Barbara kicked off a campaign of Armenian terrorism in the United States that continues today. After luring Turkish Consul Mehmet Baydor and his assistant, Bahadir Demir to the Biltmore, a seventy-seven-year-old Armenian named Gourgen Gianikian pulled out a handgun and fatally shot the diplomats.

Armenian terrorists worldwide are seeking retribution for the genocide of 1.5 million Armenians by Turkey in 1915 and the loss of their homeland. Gianikian was the sole survivor of a twenty-six-member family allegedly murdered by the Turks. Upon his arrest Gianikian avowed: "I am a prisoner of the war waged against Turkey."

Since the Biltmore Hotel assassinations, two Armenian groups, the Armenian Secret Army for the Liberation of Armenia (ASALA) and the Justice Commandos of the Armenian Genocide (JCAG), have been responsible for twenty-five terrorist incidents in the United States including assassinations in California and Massachusetts.

Like most of the home-grown and foreign terrorist groups operating in the United States, the Armenian groups utilize American-born and naturalized American citizens in their operations. The FBI arrested Steven Dadaian, an American-born member of JCAG, in a Boston hotel room. At Logan Airport, Dadaian left a suitcase that contained a timing device, blasting caps, and five sticks of dynamite.

Limited only by their imaginations, terrorists have planted bombs behind hotel walls, in hotel furniture, and in trash cans, flower pots, and food carts. Bombs at hotels have also been concealed in fire extinguishers, laundry carts, suitcases, and briefcases, and in a variety of vehicles including taxis, limousines, delivery trucks, rental cars, and airline buses.

Powerful terrorist bombs have detonated in crowded hotel lobbies, ballrooms, guests' rooms, restaurants, hallways, stairwells, and elevators. Deadly explosive devices have been planted in hotel conference rooms, restrooms, parking lots, and bars. Bombs have also detonated on hotel roofs, on balconies, and in underground garages.

Elderly operatives, fake police, phony delivery personnel, male and female couples, and terrorists pretending to be workmen have delivered explosive devices to hotels. At one heavily guarded hotel, a female terrorist smuggled a bomb beneath a maternity dress.

In most known cases, however, bombers either checked into the targeted hotel as a guest or simply put a bomb in a suitcase, walked into the hotel lobby, and walked out empty-handed.

The owner of the River Oaks Hotel in Melbourne, Florida, had a bad feeling about one of his guests who seemed befuddled and preoccupied. "There was something weird about him," the hotel owner told the *Miami Herald*.

When the sixty-nine-year-old guest checked in on January 11, 1997, carrying a suitcase and a satchel, he was out of breath and looked exhausted. The owner offered to carry both bags to the room but the guest would not allow anyone near his satchel.

"He wouldn't let go of it," the owner told the *Herald*. "It was untouchable."

The guest paid his bill in cash each day. He also walked around his room naked with the door wide open.

"You ain't one of them terrorists are you?" the hotel owner asked the guest. The owner got his answer a few days later.

Telling the owner, "I have something to do in New York," the guest checked out of the hotel but said he'd be back in a few days.

In New York the guest rode to the top of the Empire State Building and opened fire on a crowd of tourists. A sixty-nine-year-old Palestinian teacher named Ali Hassan Abu Kamal, he killed one person, wounded six others, and then turned the gun on himself. The deranged gunman had sought revenge for the treatment of Palestinians by the United States and Israel.

Terrorists frequently learn that their target is visiting a particular hotel through media reports or corridor gossip, or from hotel employees who wittingly or unwittingly provide information. In 1985, State Department Agent Jim Nagel and other law enforcement personnel from the FBI and New Orleans Police Department, arrested four armed Indian males who were conspiring to assassinate the chief minister from the Indian state of Haryana. Although the protectee's location was supposed to have been secret, the would-be assassins had a map with the minister's hotel circled.

Paul Franklin had planned to kill civil rights leader Jesse Jackson in 1982, but while listening to the radio, he learned that Vernon Jordan would be staying at an Indiana Marriott and giving a speech there. The racist shifted his sights to Jordan and shot the civil rights leader in the back as Jordan got out of his car in the Marriott's parking lot. A jury acquitted Franklin of wounding Jordan, but in 1996, while serving a life sentence for other crimes, he admitted his guilt. Jordan survived and now practices law.

* * *

One lesson I learned over and over during my travels is that the terrorist tactics used in foreign countries sooner or later show up in the United States. A person aware of a tactic is less likely to become a victim of that tactic. Many hotel employees and guests have been unwittingly exploited by terrorists. In a still-classified case in the Middle East, a terrorist duped a bellhop into delivering a briefcase bomb to a guest's room. "Would you please take my briefcase to room 706," said the terrorist as he handed the bellhop currency equivalent to 100 U.S. dollars. The anti-American terrorist was not even registered at the hotel.

The Jordanian boyfriend of a London Hilton Hotel chambermaid gave her a suitcase to carry into Heathrow Airport, but what Anne Marie Murphy didn't know was that it had a false bottom in which Nezar Hindawi had concealed a bomb. The boyfriend's intended target was an Israeli airliner.

Police acted on information that an alert receptionist at the London Visitors Hotel had provided and arrested Hindawi. The Jordanian admitted during police interrogations that Syrian air crews had smuggled guns and explosives into Britain. Syrian intelligence officers had used London's Royal Garden Hotel as their base, and Hindawi confessed that he had learned how to prime the suitcase bomb there. The hotel management was aghast.

Even if a hotel is not directly targeted, the bombs being assembled and transported by terrorists pose a great risk to the building. I know of twenty-three cases worldwide in which bombs have accidentally detonated in hotels, often killing the terrorists and innocent guests and causing millions of dollars in damages.

On July 13, 1996, an explosion and a fire in Edmond, Oklahoma, destroyed a room at the Red Carpet Motel, forcing forty-two guests to be evacuated. Kelly Sean Spenser, the occupant of the room, was hospitalized with minor injuries and then jailed after police discovered four pipe bombs and sixteen pounds of explosives in his room.

Terrorists frequently apply for employment at targeted hotels, and most large hotels have hundreds of employees who are naturally sympathetic to a wide variety of political ideologies. A violent insider poses a dangerous threat to security. Two days before Stavros Sykopetritis attempted to kill Bulent Ecevit at the Waldorf Astoria Hotel, the gunman took a job as a cashier at another New York hotel. Since the latter hotel had catered to Turkish officials in the past, Sykopetritis was simply trying to get close to his enemy.

On January 1, 1997, the Secret Service arrested a twenty-one-year-old hotel waiter who threatened President Clinton during the president's vacation on Hilton Head Island, South Carolina.

Assassinations in hotels only tell part of the story: More than 260 terrorists in the United States have used hotel rooms to hide out, to store and assemble bombs, and to plan outside attacks. In 1987, Diplomatic Security Service agents learned that a man had departed Boston en route to Washington, D.C., to kill the secretary of state. The man was arrested in his hotel room where his cache of weapons included an AR-15 rifle and two shotguns, one of which was illegally sawed off.

Although there have been a myriad of political shootings in hotels worldwide, terrorist bombs threaten greater harm and are the most common terrorist tactic used in that environment. From 1968 to 1997, terrorists detonated bombs in at least 233 hotels worldwide. In 1985, I was staying at the Sheraton Hotel in Santiago, Chile, when a car bomb demolished part of the building. My partner Tim Dixon, then the Regional Security Officer (RSO) in Chile, had asked me to come to Santiago to brief Chilean police and military personnel on tactics that were currently being used by terrorists and drug traffickers.

Ironically, two of the topics I was discussing were "vehicle bombs" and "attacks on hotels."

"I guess the bad guys wanted to give you a proper welcome," Dixon kidded.

Two incidents, which occurred thirty-eight years apart in Israel and England, best illustrate the bombing threat to hotels.

At 12:37 P.M. on July 22, 1946, a monstrous explosion at the King David Hotel in Jerusalem shook the city and launched a campaign of hotel bombings that continues to this day. Members of the right-wing Jewish Irgun, a group then led by Menachim Begin, who would later become the Israeli prime minister, planted 500 pounds of TNT and gelignite in the basement of the King David. The explosion killed ninety-one Arab, British, and Jewish guests, wounded forty-five others, and collapsed all six stories of the hotel. A bus passing in front of the hotel was blown off course and every passenger was injured. The blast propelled a Jewish pedestrian who had been standing in front of the hotel across the street into a building, killing him.

The King David, which served as the British military headquarters, was surrounded with fortresslike security. Barbed wire encircled the building. Soldiers patrolled the perimeter. Manned machine gun nests were on the roof. A security netting prevented hand grenades from being thrown through the windows, and armed guards and steel shutters barred the entrances.

Despite all the security, Irgun operatives discovered the weak link in the building's defense: the unprotected basement running the entire length of the hotel.

Shortly before noon, several Irgun men disguised themselves in Arab garb and drove up to the kitchen entrance. They unloaded a cargo of milk cans and delivered them to the hotel's Regence Cafe. No one suspected that the milk cans concealed explosives. The phony deliverymen held the kitchen staff hostage, planted the explosives in the basement, and murdered a British officer and a policeman who stumbled upon the operation.

Thirty-eight years later, the Provisional Irish Republican Army (PIRA)—a group that has operated in the United States—hoped to assassinate then Prime Minister Margaret Thatcher and the entire British Cabinet. PIRA planted a powerful "sleeper" bomb behind paneling in a seventh-floor bathroom of the Grand Hotel in Brighton, England. A sleeper bomb is designed to detonate days or even months after being placed.

On October 12, 1984, the PIRA sleeper woke up.

The bomb demolished a large portion of the hotel, killed three politicians and the wife of another, and wounded thirty-four other people. Prime Minister Thatcher escaped injury, but the blast totally destroyed a bathroom she had used moments earlier in her first floor suite.

In claiming credit for the spectacular bombing, the Provisional Irish Republican Army noted: "Today we were unlucky. But remember, we have only to be lucky once; you have to be lucky always."

CHAPTER

9

Unaffiliated and Indiscriminate

Loners on the Rampage

ONE DAY IN 1966, CHARLES WHITMAN, A FORMER Marine and a student at the University of Texas at Austin, filled a footlocker with seven shoulder weapons, three handguns, four knives, and 1,200 rounds of ammunition. Whitman climbed to the top of the 307-foot Texas Tower on the campus and began a shooting rampage that lasted ninety-seven minutes before an Austin police officer stopped the crazed gunman for good. Sixteen people died; thirty-three were wounded. Strewn with casualties, the campus looked much like a battlefield.

James Oliver Huberty, armed with a shotgun, a handgun, and a semiautomatic rifle, charged into a crowded McDonald's fast-food restaurant in San Diego on July 18, 1984, and shouted: "I'm going to kill you all!" Huberty slew twenty-one people and wounded nineteen before police sniper Officer Charles Foster took him out.

James Edward Pough walked into the General Motors Acceptance Corporation in Jacksonville, Florida, on June 18, 1990, carrying a .30-caliber semiautomatic rifle and a .38-caliber revolver, and shot at eighty-six workers seated in row upon row of desks. Pough seriously wounded four employees and killed ten others before killing himself.

To develop better defenses and responses to mass-casualty attacks, counterterrorism experts study rampage shootings by both nonpolitical mentally unstable individuals and politically motivated terrorists. Such shootings have accounted for hundreds of casualties in the United States.

Perhaps the most dangerous assassin in our midst and the one most difficult to guard against is the loner who has no police record of violent behavior, who has no affiliation with known groups that advocate violence, and who indiscriminately inflicts violence upon innocent people. Armed with powerful, easily accessible weapons that fire more than 600 rounds per minute, today's terrorist is capable of turning crowded airports, athletic events, and other assemblies into slaughterhouses. A single gun in the hands of a loner can be calamitous.

On September 22, 1975, as President Ford exited the St. Francis Hotel in San Francisco, Sara Jane Moore fired a single shot from a .38-caliber revolver, narrowly missing the president before security personnel subdued and arrested her. Moore's assassination attempt on the president of the United States finally earned her the attention she so desperately desired. A one-time informer for the Federal Bureau of Investigation (FBI), Moore had been seeking approval of friends within the leftist radical community. A judge sentenced her to life in prison. She escaped for a short while and was recaptured. Speaking of her assassination attempt outside the St. Francis Hotel, Moore stated, "I wish I had killed him. I did it to create chaos."

Testimony during the 1997 trial of Timothy McVeigh, the man subsequently convicted of the Oklahoma City bombing, strongly suggests that he, too, wanted to create chaos.

On March 30, 1981, John W. Hinckley worked his way into the crowd of reporters and photographers standing behind a security rope at a side entrance to the Washington Hilton Hotel. The press was waiting for President Ronald Reagan and his entourage to emerge from the hotel. As the president strode toward his waiting limousine, Hinckley dropped a camera he had been using as a prop and started blasting away with a handgun, hitting Reagan, Press Secretary James Brady, policeman Thomas Delahanty, and Secret Service Agent Timothy McCarthy. Hinckley intended his actions to impress actress Jodie Foster. She was horrified.

The "media masquerade" tactic used by Hinckley outside the Washington Hilton has been used by dozens of terrorists worldwide to commit assassinations, deliver bombs, kidnap celebrities, and enter secure areas.

The most infamous lone terrorist associated with educational institutions was the "Unabomber," so named because his first victims were professors at universities. The handcrafted and painstakingly made exploding wooden boxes allegedly made by the Unabomber killed three people and wounded twenty-nine others between May 1978 and April 1995. He mailed deadly parcel bombs to fourteen separate locations in the United States, including eight to universities or university personnel. Charles Epstein, a geneticist at the University of California-San Francisco, lost several fingers when a package exploded in his home. Another Unabomber device severely wounded David Gelernter, a computer scientist at Yale University, in the abdomen, chest, face, and hands. A bomb seriously injured a secretary who opened the parcel for a professor at Vanderbilt University. Other targets were affiliated with the University of Utah, Northwestern University, the University of Michigan, and the University of California-Berkeley.

While reading the Unabomber's "manifesto," which the *New York Times* and the *Washington Post* jointly published, hermit Theodore J. Kaczynski's brother recognized phrasings that sounded similar to Ted's letters to home. Montana police arrested Ted Kaczynski, a former math professor at the University of California, and charged him with murder.

Another loner eluded capture for four years despite an international manhunt. A week before going on a shooting spree in Virginia in 1993, terrorist Mir Aimal Kansi, a twenty-eight-year-old Pakistani and devout Muslim, told his roommate that he was angry about the treatment of Muslims in Bosnia and that he was going to get even by shooting up the Central Intelligence Agency (CIA), the White House, or the Israeli embassy. At that time, Serb nationalist forces had seized control of about 75 percent of Bosnia, mostly at the expense of Muslims. Pursuing an "ethnic cleansing" campaign to drive out Muslims, Bosnian Serbs participated in rape, torture, and genocide on a scale that dwarfed anything seen in Europe since Nazi times.

On January 18, 1993, Kansi, using a mail-order catalogue, purchased a bullet-resistant vest from Matthews Police Supply Company near Charlotte, North Carolina. (I always use the term bullet-"resistant" vest because there is no such thing as a bullet-"proof" vest. On one assignment in the mountains of El Salvador, I hung my government-issued bulletproof vest on a tree limb and, using a captured guerrilla weapon, fired eight rounds into it. Six of the eight rounds penetrated the vest and embedded deeply into a tree.) On January 22, he purchased an AK-47-type rifle from the David Condon, Inc., gun store in Chantilly, Virginia. The deadly AK-47, which can fire ten powerful rounds a second, has long been the weapon of choice for many international terrorists.

The next morning, Kansi drove to CIA headquarters in Langley, Virginia, and parked his car on the side of the road. He walked over to drivers stopped at a red light on Dolly Madison Boulevard who were waiting to turn left into the main entrance of the CIA. Raising his powerful weapon, Kansi fired at five motorists. In a matter of seconds, CIA employees Frank Darling, twenty-eight, and Lansing H. Bennett, sixty-six, were dead, and three other CIA employees were permanently injured.

Like so many other assassins in the United States, Kansi was able to depart the country as easily as he had entered. He landed in Pakistan thirty-six hours after the shootings.

Coming from a very wealthy family, Kansi had many people, including some government employees, who were willing to help him escape justice. Kansi's clan belongs to the minority Pashtun people, many of whom live in neighboring Afghanistan. Most of Kansi's immediate family lives in Quetta, a remote, dangerous area of Pakistan I know very well. They own two hotels, three restaurants, apartment buildings, orchards, and other real estate.

Kansi has a graduate degree in English: He is not a stupid man. He knew we would never give up. He knew that the $2-million reward the United States put on his head would tempt a lot of people. He knew that one day when he least expected it, when he was feeling the most comfortable, U.S. agents would appear out of nowhere and get him.

The breakthrough in the search came on June 3, 1997, when Afghan sources told CIA agents they were in contact with Kansi. The Afghans offered to lure Kansi to a hotel under the pretense of conducting a business deal with him.

At 4:00 A.M., on June 15, 1997, a sudden knock at the door roused Kansi from a sound sleep in a seedy Afghan hotel near the Pakistan border. Four FBI agents, including two members of their elite special weapons and tactics (SWAT) team, stood armed and ready in the dark, run-down hallway outside of Kansi's room. A fifth agent stood guard fifteen feet away. When Kansi groggily responded to the knock on the door, alone and unprepared, the agents burst in and slammed him to the floor. The assassin cursed the agents, first in Pathaw and then in English, but he quieted when he saw the gun pointed at his head. The thirty-three-year-old native of Pakistan who had bragged about killing the CIA agents and wounding three other Americans had been captured by a coalition of CIA operatives, FBI and State Department agents, Pakistani spies, and Afghan warriors.

After his predawn arrest, Kansi was shoved into a waiting four-wheel drive vehicle, driven to a remote airstrip, hustled aboard a camouflaged U.S. Air Force C-141 transport plane, and flown to Dulles International Airport. His long-delayed appointment with justice had begun.

* * *

The United States is not the only victim of loners who have carried out multiple murder rampages. A deranged U.S. citizen named Baruch Goldstein, who was visiting the West Bank, put on an Israeli military uniform and opened fire inside a crowded mosque where hundreds of innocent Palestinians were praying. The American killed 30 Arabs and wounded 155.

CHAPTER

10

Tips and Tricks

Deciphering Information

ON SEPTEMBER 11, 1980, A NEW YORK POLICE DE-partment (NYPD) undercover detective and I drove the streets of Manhattan to interview a man who had threatened a Cuban diplomat. The target was one of three Cubans under State Department protection while they attended the United Nations General Assembly. All three diplomats had been marked by terrorists.

"I'm going to rid the world of the menace," the threat-maker wrote in a letter, "and shout [sic] him between the eyes and shout [sic] him in the heart."

In the diplomatic protection business, agents have to check out every threat, whether from terrorist groups or loners, regardless of spelling or grammar.

Every time the undercover officer and I reached within a few blocks of the potential "shouter," the car radio crackled an officer-in-distress call. We assisted dozens of police cars responding to three such calls at three different locations. A flood of false reports to 911 was also sending patrol cars all over Manhattan.

"What's going on?" the detective hollered into his microphone.

Seeing all the police cars, I surmised that someone was intentionally diverting our attention. Then came the announcement: Gunmen had slain a Cuban diplomat near his automobile in the opposite direction of the officer-in-distress and bogus 911 calls. The Black Liberation Army (BLA) and other groups in the United States had used the ruse in the past. This time the anti-Castro group Omega-7 made the calls.

Omega-7 gunmen assassinated Felix Garcia-Rodriguez, an attaché to the Cuban Mission at the United Nations, on a busy New York street. The deceased had left me with the impression that he was a womanizer and a hothead. Since he frequented certain disco bars after work, Omega-7 probably didn't have much trouble tailing him or determining his routine. The position of his body indicated that the diplomat was probably stepping out of his vehicle when the assassins shot him. They may have called out an insult to lure him into the open.

Hours later, the detective and I finally arrived at the letter-writer's apartment to search for possible leads. A 400-pound, thirty-six-year-old man greeted us at the door, completely naked except for a belt and one sock. He lived with his elderly mother and had been in and out of mental institutions. In one hand he held a copy of the *National Inquirer;* the other gripped an empty video box. A gruesome horror movie played on the TV set.

"Hope we're not interrupting anything important," the detective said.

"Come on in," invited the man, his mouth stuffed with food. "We've got company, Mama."

A passive, sad-looking woman wandered in from the kitchen. The apartment reeked of excrement.

"Are you planning on 'shouting' someone?" I asked the man. Looking at me quizzically, he answered that he planned to shoot "those foreign bastards between the eyes and in the heart."

The law allowed us to commit the odd man for evaluation, so we convinced him to attach some pants to his belt and escorted him to a state mental hospital. A woman in a white coat cheerfully said, "Hi, Bob. It's good to see you again."

The hospital released the man into his mother's custody thirty days later. He never "shouted" at any of our protectees, but two years later he did shoot his mama—shot her between the eyes and in the heart.

* * *

All law enforcement officers trying to counter terrorism consume as much information as possible about violent groups such as Omega-7 and their allies. Knowledge is power, after all. Every scrap of information, every puzzle piece helps develop a picture of the enemy. Sometimes, however, there are extra pieces in the box.

Eighteen months before Omega-7 gunned down Felix Garcia-Rodriguez, they bombed Kennedy International Airport. Almost immediately I sought individuals who could help me build a profile of the anti-Castro group for the State Department's protection teams.

I met a Cuban-American undercover officer with a Florida police department who had infiltrated one of the anti-Castro groups. His father had been a political prisoner in Cuba and openly advocated the assassination of Castro. The elderly man spat at the TV set any time Castro's name was mentioned.

"My biggest fear is that we will arrest a bunch of assassins and my father will be one of them," the officer laughed.

He told me that Omega-7 wanted him to obtain radio scanners and police uniforms, badges, and credentials from New York and Florida.

Another law enforcement officer, Agent Carter Cornick of the Federal Bureau of Investigation's (FBI) headquarters in Washington, D.C., added more to the terrorists' picture. Cornick laid out the intricacies of the 1976 assassination of Chilean Ambassador Orlando Letelier and Omega-7's involvement. Letelier drove his American assistant Ronni Moffitt to work one day through Washington's morning rush hour. Her husband Michael sat behind them in the back seat. As they rounded the bronze statue of Civil War General Philip Sheridan astride his horse, Winchester, in the heart of Embassy Row, a bomb planted beneath the ambassador's car detonated, blowing off Letelier's legs. Ronni Moffitt stumbled from the car onto the grass and drowned in her own blood while her husband yelled for help, screaming, "Assassins! Assassins!"

According to Cornick, the Chilean intelligence service recruited Michael Townley, an American citizen and possible genius, who, in turn, committed state-directed assassinations in Argentina, Chile, and Italy. Townley had enlisted three Omega-7 members to help him with the Letelier murder.

"Omega-7 isn't the brightest bunch I've ever investigated, but they're incredibly brazen," Cornick warned. And dangerous because of it.

An image of the terrorist group was emerging.

When Omega-7 threatened our three Cuban protectees, I appealed to New York-based FBI Agent Larry Wack for any information that would give our agents the upper hand. He handed me a stack of surveillance photographs and said, "These are the guys I'm most concerned about."

The anti-Castro Cuban underground had many sympathizers in New York who might abet them, sympathizers employed as taxi drivers and security guards or who worked at hotels, airports, or government buildings. Two men arrested at an anti-Castro demonstration were employed at a restaurant that my protectees often visited: one waited tables; the other parked cars.

"These guys are good bomb-makers but don't forget they are always training with firearms," warned Agent Wack. "I suspect they'll come out shooting." The murder of Garcia-Rodriguez proved him right.

* * *

One of the twenty-five predictions I made in 1983 for the Washington area law enforcement community, based solely on analysis, was that routine traffic stops by police officers would prove to be one of our most valuable counterterrorist weapons. Between 1977 and 1997, police officers encountered eighty-eight domestic and international terrorists while making routine traffic stops. The price was high: At least sixteen police officers were killed or wounded during these encounters.

On April 12, 1988, a New Jersey State Trooper, Robert Cieplensky, noticed an Asian man acting suspiciously at a rest station on the New Jersey Turnpike. The man took off when he saw the trooper, but Cieplensky caught him and found in the car three antipersonnel pipe bombs—modified fire extinguisher cylinders filled with gunpowder, bird shot, and other shrapnel. Cieplensky also confiscated fifteen pounds of black powder, a false passport, $3,600 in $100 bills, and a Swiss bank account card.

The man's name was Yu Kikumura, and he was a member of the violent Japanese Red Army (JRA). Investigators believe he had planned to detonate the bombs at a U.S. military installation on April 15, 1988, the second anniversary of the U.S. retaliatory air strike on Tripoli. Not coincidentally, the JRA planted a bomb two days after Kikumura's arrest outside the USO club in Naples, Italy, killing five people, including an American servicewoman.

While driving his beat, Interstate 35, on April 19, 1995, Oklahoma Highway Patrolman Charlie Hanger saw a battered, yellow Mercury Marquis with a rusted bumper. The car had no license plate. Trooper Hanger pulled over the Marquis at 10:15 A.M., one hour and fifteen minutes after a massive bomb leveled the Alfred P. Murrah Federal Building in Oklahoma City. The trooper noticed a bulge beneath the man's coat, which turned out to be a .9-millimeter semiautomatic Glock. Trooper Hanger arrested the driver, Timothy J. McVeigh, on weapons charges and five misdemeanors.

The next day, one hour before McVeigh was to be released on bond, the FBI called the Oklahoma Highway Patrol and told them that McVeigh was a suspect in the bombing of the Murrah building. A Social Security number that Trooper Hanger had transmitted to the national police crime database tipped off the federal agents.

A routine traffic stop had yielded a mass murderer.

Four days before Christmas in 1981, New Jersey State Trooper Philip Lamonaco pulled over two men in a blue Chevy Nova with Connecticut license plates. He spotted a handgun in the car, confiscated it, and ordered the men out of the vehicle. As the driver got out of the car, his hands in the air, he began arguing and yelling. The other man emerged from the passenger side and fired fourteen rounds from a .9-millimeter semiautomatic handgun. Lamonaco's bullet-resistant vest stopped most of the high-speed slugs but one penetrated beneath his armpit and slashed into his heart. Mortally wounded, Lamonaco fired six rounds as he collapsed to the ground, missing the two men but hitting the Nova three times. The two men sped away in the Chevy, leaving Lamonaco bleeding to death in the snow.

A massive manhunt ensued, eventually leading to the capture of an anti-imperialist, prison-reform group called the Sam Melville–Jonathan Jackson Brigade, an elusive terrorist organization that had bombed seven buildings, including a courthouse, and had robbed several banks.

In another seemingly simple traffic case, two police officers in Queens, New York, stopped a van in April 1981. Two BLA members exited the van shooting, hitting one officer fourteen times in the legs and back and the other, in the jaw, the right ear, and a leg.

The BLA was one of the five groups that attacked a Brink's truck in New York on October 20, 1981, stealing nearly $1.6 million in cash and killing two police officers and a Brink's guard.

As of June 1997, the BLA is considered viable but inactive. Several members have joined new groups, some are still fugitives, and some incarcerated members are still talking "revolution."

* * *

One of the most helpful tools in all areas of law enforcement is citizen involvement. Even the fictional Sherlock Holmes needed clues to solve his cases.

A resident of Evanston, Illinois, a quiet, upper-class Chicago suburb, called police on April 4, 1980, to report that a group of men and women wearing jogging outfits were climbing in and out of a van parked in front of his home. He thought it strange. The citizen also thought it odd that the joggers chain-smoked cigarettes and had placed a radio antenna on the van's roof.

At 3:30 P.M. officers Patrick Lenart, Red Lamberdin, Mike Gillespie, Douglas Glanz, and Torbin Nielsen reached the citizen's home in separate squad cars and blocked in the tan-colored van. Curtains covered the vehicle's rear windows; a drape hung behind the front seats, obscuring the view to the rear compartment. The van had no side windows.

As Officer Lenart approached the van, a Latino woman in the driver's seat hurriedly rolled up her window, started the engine, and put the van in gear. As he ordered her to turn off the engine, Lenart observed her fumbling with her purse. By then, Officer Lamberdin stood at the front passenger door.

When someone behind the Latino woman gently tugged the drape aside to eye the goings-on, Officer Nielsen saw more people in the back compartment and ordered everyone out. With weapons drawn, the officers positioned some of the nine men and women against a nearby fence and some against the van.

At that point, Officer Nielsen searched the driver's purse and uncovered a .9-millimeter automatic weapon. He also saw a wig, false sideburns, and a CB radio in the van's front seat area. Officer Gillespie found several shotguns in the van. From one of the women, Officer Glanz confiscated a blue canvas bag containing additional firearms.

While interviewing one of the male suspects, Officer Nielsen noticed that the man was wearing a full set of street clothes beneath his jogging outfit. As he questioned the suspect, the man's fake mustache fell off.

The patrolmen handcuffed the men and women and transported them to police headquarters. The suspicious characters turned out to be nine of the most-wanted Puerto Rican terrorists in U.S. history. Coincidentally, other police officers arrested two individuals the same day for stealing vans. The culprits were also members of Puerto Rico's Armed Forces of National Liberation (FALN).

The family of Henry Crown, one of the wealthiest people in America and in 1980 the head of General Dynamics Corporation, lived one block from the arrest site of the nine terrorists. It is not known if the terrorists' plan involved the Crown family, but it is known that they had planned to rob an armored bank vehicle making a pickup at a nearby university.

The citizen's call proved even more valuable when one of the eleven arrested FALN members decided to cooperate with authorities.

I interviewed Freddie Mendez and learned important and fascinating inside information concerning FALN training, tactics, and operations. A crack team of U.S. Marshals guarded him at a secret office located in an industrial park on the outskirts of Washington, D. C.

Once the FALN accepted Freddie into the organization, they ordered him to curtail his overt Puerto Rican independence activities and to appear disinterested in all political issues. They instructed him to shave his mustache, shorten his hair, dress conservatively, and hold a legitimate steady job.

"Win your boss's approval by working hard, being on time, dressing well, and being polite," they told him. Freddie attended FALN training sessions, meetings, and clandestine activities at night so that he would not arouse suspicion by missing work.

They taught Freddie to constantly change his schedule, to take indirect routes to his destination, to change modes of transportation, and to confuse police by reversing direction of travel—all precautionary actions to counter possible surveillances. "If I took a taxi, I got out a mile away from my destination," he explained.

"Be watchful of other passengers who wait with you," Freddie's terrorism instructor advised and told him to let some buses and trains pass him by. He wore reversible jackets and hats, wigs, false beards, and eyeglasses to disguise himself.

Freddie told me that one male FALN member convincingly dressed as a female on some assignments. One Catholic bomber affected a Yiddish accent, wore a yarmulke, and lived in a Jewish neighborhood. A dark-skinned Puerto Rican member used a darker shade of make-up and pretended to be of African descent.

FALN members learned to scheme, to lie bald-faced, to use their ingratiating wiles. One member smeared fake blood on his face and shirt as he rode an elevator to the top floor of an office building. Feigning a bloody nose, the man pinched his nostrils closed, tilted his head backwards, and politely asked the startled receptionist, "May I use the bathroom to clean up?" The FALN had previously surveilled their target and knew the executives' bathroom was locked and off limits to the public. Freddie explained that his group studied the inside of secured buildings by taking advantage of public tours or by pretending to be students or researchers in need of information. "We'd go to the interview and then roam around as we pleased."

The guileless receptionist ignored policy and provided a restroom key to the bloodied terrorist. Once inside, the man unstrapped a pipe bomb from his ankle and concealed it behind the commode. After cleaning the blood off his face, he thanked the receptionist and departed. Fortunately, no one was inside the stall when the bomb blew up.

A female FALN member gained access to a locked executive bathroom by requesting to change her baby's diaper. The receptionist initially hesitated, so the woman placed her baby in public view on an expensive leather couch. "Okay, okay! It would be better if you did that in the restroom," the receptionist decided.

Freddie wasn't sure whether the "mother" had concealed the bomb beneath the baby stroller or in the baby's diaper.

According to the data, terrorists plant more than 100 bombs in public restrooms each year, worldwide.

He said some members would desensitize or try to become familiar to security guards. "At first you might just say hello to the guard. After a while you engage him in some conversation. Then you might ask if he wants a cup of coffee," Freddie explained. "Gradually the guard gets to know you, thinks you are okay, and eventually views you as a nonthreat."

Freddie said he had the impression that the group had plenty of money. He was probably right. The FALN robbed banks, movie theaters, and armored cars, skimmed money from government-sponsored programs, and even embezzled money from religious organizations. At least seven FALN members joined the National Commission on Hispanic Affairs, a group set up by the Episcopal Church, to channel millions of dollars to Hispanic groups. The FALN members engineered approximately $100,000 in fraudulent grants from the commission and disappeared with the money.

During one armored car robbery in Milwaukee, Wisconsin, an FALN member who had dressed as a postman, pretended to be using the telephone in front of a grocery store. As the guard exited the store with a bag of cash, the "postman" put a gun to his ribs and stole the money. An accomplice who had been preposted in the supermarket was accidentally left behind. When the police arrived, the accomplice made a purchase, casually walked past them, and escaped.

Freddie was a reluctant revolutionary. His motivation in joining the FALN had more to do with peer pressure and personal problems than with politics. Finding it difficult to hate America, he was more interested in adventure and "belonging" than he was in independence for Puerto Rico.

"Many members could not speak Spanish and had never been to Puerto Rico."

I was naturally very interested in the FALN's intelligence-gathering capabilities. Judging from the advanced tactics and procedures the FALN was using, it appeared to me that some members had been directly trained by the Cuban intelligence service.

In addition to the personnel files stolen during the January 14, 1980, National Guard Armory attack in Wisconsin, the FALN had collected detailed data on more than 100 U.S. citizens. FALN intelligence files included surveillance photographs of U.S. attorneys and law enforcement agents who were working against them. Freddie told me that my name had been brought up at a clandestine meeting and that he recalled having seen my name in a newspaper article. The group utilized "dead drops" to contact one another, and they communicated in code.

Many FALN members and sympathizers worked in jobs and professions that would assist their terrorist endeavors. Members who worked at a university in Illinois provided information for a planned armored car robbery at that school. At least six FALN members were suspected of being in the U.S. armed services. "One guy bragged about being in charge of security at a military base," said Freddie. "Another member lived with a woman who worked for a police department."

The average FALN member is a man or a woman who does not fit any Hollywood terrorist profile. And nobody knows this better than the people who live in the neighborhood of Squirrel Hill, Pennsylvania.

Melting into the middle-class neighborhood, the man who called himself Greg Peters and the woman known as Jo Elliott were viewed as doting parents, helpful friends, and community volunteers. The people of Squirrel Hill often ran into Greg and Jo at neighborhood cookouts or when they took their children trick-or-treating during Halloween.

But the people of Squirrel Hill had never seen the photographs of Greg and Jo on the FBI's "Ten Most Wanted" posters. "Terrorists," the wanted posters proclaimed in big letters. "Do not approach—armed and dangerous."

Greg and Jo, as the neighbors referred to them, were actually Claude Daniel Marks, forty-five, and Donna Jean Willmott, forty-four, two former members of the radical Weather Underground Organization (WUO).

The WUO, which has long been linked to Puerto Rican terrorist groups, carried out a violent terrorist campaign in the United States that began in the late 1960s and didn't end until the mid-1980s. On March 1, 1971, exactly seventeen years after Puerto Rican nationalists attacked the U.S. House of Representatives, the WUO detonated a bomb at the U.S. Capitol to protest U.S. military activities in Laos. In addition to that bombing, the Weathermen hit forty other targets including the U.S. Department of State and the Pentagon, the latter bombing causing $800,000 in damages. On October 20, 1981, members of five domestic terrorist groups—Weathermen among them—formed an alliance, attacked a Brinks armored truck in New York, and stole $1,589,000. Three innocent people died and three others were wounded. Some WUO members are still wanted fugitives.

Like many Puerto Rican terrorists, several Weathermen traveled and trained in Cuba. The Marxist FALN has close ties to Cuba but it is not, as yet, a Cuban puppet. And like the WUO, the FALN sometimes does favors for other groups in hopes that the favor will someday be returned. On September 20, 1982, Puerto Rican terrorists exploded a bomb at a New York bank "to protest the killing of Palestinians in Beirut."

Marks, a onetime radio journalist, and Willmott, a former acupuncturist and medical assistant, were arrested in Squirrel Hill in 1994 and accused of plotting to blow up Leavenworth Federal Penitentiary in Kansas. FALN operatives were to land a helicopter in the confusion, fire on any guards who interfered, and spring FALN leader Oscar Lopez.

For their part in the escape plot, Willmott and Marks were sentenced to prison terms on March 9, 1995.

Freddie Mendez was taught that if he ever went to jail, his duty was to recruit new members and to teach them bomb-making skills and other tricks of the terrorist trade. Instead, he provided a lode of information to the law enforcement community.

In another case of routine police work, NYPD officers and FBI agents probably thwarted a potentially lethal crime. Acting on a tip from an informant on July 31, 1997, authorities charged into a Brooklyn apartment and confiscated bombs made of pipes, gunpowder, nails, and toggle switches that could have killed everyone within a thirty-foot enclosed radius.

Police also found anti-Israel literature, a portrait of Sheik Omar Abdul Rahman (the militant Egyptian cleric who was convicted of a plot to bomb the United Nations and other targets), and a possible draft of a suicide note. Officials allege that the two men, Palestinians Ghazi Abu Maizar and Lafi Khalil, had intended to commit a suicide bombing attack on a busy subway station and a commuter bus.

Neither of the alleged terrorists should have been in the United States at the time of their arrests. Abu Maizar made his way to New York after having been arrested three times attempting to enter the United States illegally from Canada. After his third arrest, an immigration judge set him free and reduced his bond from $15,000 to $5,000.

Lafi Khalil entered the United States legally but lapsed into illegal status. Under the terms of his visitor's visa he should have left the country eight months before his arrest.

* * *

Every now and then, law enforcement gets to ply a few tricks of its own trade.

A source who had always provided reliable information told me that the elusive, unidentified bomb-maker we were seeking would be taking the 10:00 A.M. train. I can't say where or when. The details are still classified.

We didn't know what the man looked like, or even if the bomb-maker were a man, but we were intimately aware of someone's lethal handiwork. Six bombs had already detonated in office buildings, an embassy, and a police station, killing three people and wounding twenty-three others. Police found three other pipe bombs inside a stolen van that they had pulled over for "driving too slowly." The female driver ran faster than she drove and got away. It was a hot summer day and the officer distinctly remembers that the woman was wearing gloves. Four other pipe bombs were hastily left behind in a safehouse after a police insider tipped off the terrorists that their apartment was about to be raided. We were 99 percent sure that the same person had assembled all thirteen pipe bombs.

All the members of this bomb-maker's team were professionals. Not one usable fingerprint was discovered in the van or the safehouse. They must have worn gloves at all times. No prints on the toilet handle, light bulbs, silverware, or glasses. No prints on any piece of garbage, the lamps, adjustable shower nozzle, or the back of a dozen unused postage stamps that they left behind. We did find some cat and human hairs, a tube of a prescription ointment that herpes sufferers use, and a half-eaten chocolate-covered cookie with a clear, identifiable bite impression. Fibers in the chocolate probably came from a glove.

I was credited with coming up with the plan to disguise a bomb-sniffing canine as a Seeing-Eye dog to hunt for the bomb-maker on the 10:00 A.M. train, but I had gotten the idea from a cheap detective novel.

We bought a pair of dark glasses and a white cane for Carlos, the half-Spanish, half-Irish officer who worked with Jessie, the half-German Shepherd, half-who-knows-what bomb-sniffing dog. We outfitted Jessie with a spiffy Seeing-Eye dog harness. She and Carlos made a cute couple.

"Now remember, you can't see," I instructed Carlos.

We took Jessie to the safehouse so she could train her nose to the relevant scents, and she picked up traces of explosives on the dining room table, on the carpet, and on the sofa. She rolled on the sofa and the carpet and licked the table.

The next morning, officers concealed at all the train stations were secretly videotaping every passenger entering and exiting the 10:00 A.M. train.

It was a long shot, but our plan was to let Carlos and Jessie walk the aisles of the train looking for our bomb-maker. Carlos was to tap his white cane and hold onto Jessie's harness.

"And make sure the passengers can't see your gun!" I reminded Carlos.

We told Jessie to sniff out any passenger who had recently been handling explosives. As an incentive, we offered Jessie a steak if she located the bomb-maker.

Carlos and Jessie had their hands and paws full with the fifteen-car train. We had only five officers on the train, four men and one woman, but we moved from car to car as best we could without being too conspicuous, trying to make sure someone was with the "blind" man at all times.

We walked the entire length of the train with no luck, but a lot of passengers offered to help Carlos, and Jessie seemed to be having a good time. I noticed Carlos politely rejected the offers of all Good Samaritans save one: a very pretty blonde lady whom he grabbed by the arm.

Then it happened. We were in the fourth car heading back towards the front of the train. Carlos was tapping his white cane and adjusting his dark glasses when Jessie suddenly broke free, "alerted" on a disheveled man seated next to a window and clamped down tightly on the male passenger's crotch.

"Good dog!" I whispered under my breath.

Every time the embarrassed man pushed the dog away, Jessie burrowed her nose deeper and clamped down harder. He had been holding explosives on his lap within the last eighteen hours.

"Get him off of me!" the man screamed in an unusually high-pitched voice.

"It's a she," Carlos replied, acting bewildered and lost.

"Whatever," the man screamed again. "Get her away from me."

"What's happening, can someone help me please?" Carlos asked, now giving a brilliant performance. I know he hoped that the pretty blonde would rescue him but a very nice grandmotherly type intervened.

"Your dog is biting one of the passengers," the woman gently explained as she pulled Jessie away. Carlos apologized profusely to the man and thanked the lady for her help.

It was beautiful. I took a seat a few rows away, facing the passenger. The kind, elderly lady escorted Carlos to an empty seat near the restroom. He pretended to scold Jessie, who looked confused. Had she done something to lose the steak? But when they were out of the passengers' sight, Carlos hugged and patted Jessie and whispered, "Good girl." Jessie looked content: The steak was now a sure bet.

The team had already decided to surveil anyone Jessie "alerted" on, so the team leader got on the radio and made the appropriate arrangements. It was not my case, nor was it in my jurisdiction; I had been invited along because my source had come up with the lead. The team leader knew that I hated bomb-makers. A pipe bomb had killed my good friend Arleigh McCree, an Explosive Ordnance Disposal expert with the Los Angeles Police Department, and his partner Officer Ronald Ball as they approached it at a private Los Angeles home.

The female officer got lucky and was able to share a taxi with the bomb-maker. She kept him in sight until seventeen additional officers arrived and set up a twenty-four-hour surveillance. When the disheveled man returned to the area of the safehouse, the team knew for certain that Jessie had earned her steak. The bomb-maker wasn't stupid enough to go into the safehouse but it was obvious he was snooping around.

It turned out to be an intelligence gold mine. The bomb-maker unknowingly led the officers to two additional safehouses and inadvertently pointed out three other terrorists. The police made four arrests, confiscated a huge amount of explosives and a number of weapons, and certainly saved lives.

The police gave my informant $23,000 in reward money for his information but I warned them, "Don't you dare try to steal my snitch."

I contacted a mail-order steak house when I got home and sent Jessie three big, fat, juicy steaks.

CHAPTER

11

Lives on the Line

The Agents

S PECIAL AGENT TOM COLIN WORKED IN THE THICK
of terrorist turmoil in 1990. The Diplomatic Security Service (DSS) had assigned him to Santiago, Chile, where the
Manuel Rodriguez Patriotic Front/Dissidents (FPMR/D) and a
variety of other terrorist organizations detonated bombs almost daily.

Agent Colin sought a healthy diversion from sixteen-
hour work days and constant reports of death and destruction,
and joined the American Chamber of Commerce softball team.

His team had a game scheduled at Santiago's National
Stadium on November 17. The spacious arena accommodated
a host of athletes so no one was suspicious of the two men
walking over to the American team's dugout, one carrying an
aluminum bat over his shoulder. No one noticed when the
two men walked off the field, leaving the bat behind.

At 12:10 P.M. one of Agent Colin's teammates picked up
the aluminum bat, liked the feel of it, and stepped up to the
plate. The first pitch: a swing and a miss. The second: batter
swings and connects.

A deafening explosion.

Terrorists had booby-trapped the bat with explosives and packed it with screws and bolts that served as shrapnel. The blast killed a Canadian player and injured three other people, including Agent Colin, who lost an eye.

Refusing to let the injury prevent him from fighting terrorists, Agent Colin worked hard to recuperate, and on returning to work, asked, "So, where's my next assignment."

* * *

This book is dedicated to the street police officer, our first line of defense. But it also salutes the special agents assigned to the DSS and the Regional Security Officers (RSO) at the U.S. Department of State. These internationally deployed agents have had more hands-on experience with terrorists and terrorist organizations and their ambushes, bombings, assassinations, embassy takeovers, and hostage situations than any other U.S. law enforcement personnel. The unique positions of DSS agents constantly put them in the midst of the most violent conflicts in more than 100 countries. They have been taken hostage and have been killed or wounded in aircraft bombings, snipings, embassy assaults, vehicle bombs, rocket attacks, pipe bombs, letter bombs, booby-traps, and motorcade ambushes.

Despite the threats to their own lives, DSS agents have prevented many terrorist crimes and they have captured dangerous and sometimes evil men and women. Three DSS agents caught the world's most wanted terrorist in 1995: Ramzi Ahmed Yousef, the mastermind behind the 1993 World Trade Center bombing.

Agents Jeff Riner, Art Maurel, and Bill Miller and a team of Pakistani commandos arrested Yousef in Islamabad at 9:40 A.M. on February 7, 1995, blocking a high-tech plot he had already set in motion to bomb twelve U.S. jumbo jets in flight. His goal: killing 4,000 passengers.

Yousef was born on April 27, 1968, in Pakistan but grew up in Kuwait. His father, he claims, is Pakistani and his mother is Palestinian. He enrolled in Great Britain's Swansea Institute in 1986 and graduated from the Welsh university three years later with a degree in electronic engineering, a handy major for a bomb-maker.

Yousef returned to Kuwait in 1989, stayed a brief while, then traveled to the Philippine Islands in early 1991. There he made contact with Islamic militants and established a base of operations for his Far East terrorist activities.

Traveling on an Iraqi passport, Yousef arrived at John F. Kennedy International Airport in New York on September 1, 1992. Despite the arrest and incarceration of his Palestinian companion, Ahmad Mohammad Ajaj, for traveling on a false passport, the United States granted Yousef's request for asylum in which he cited "political and religious reasons."

Three days later, Yousef began living in three different Jersey City apartments with individuals who would later be identified as terrorists.

Shortly after the 1,200-pound bomb exploded at the World Trade Center, Yousef disappeared but turned up soon after in the Philippines. Shortly after a bomb exploded at the Zamboanga International Airport, he coincidentally departed the Philippines for Pakistan.

A bomb Yousef was building in his Karachi hotel room detonated prematurely on July 23, 1993. Two hospitals treated him for serious injuries to both hands and one eye, leaving him with deep, noticeable scars.

Most likely as a dress rehearsal for simultaneously blowing up the twelve U.S. planes, Yousef planted a bomb on Philippines Airline flight 434. The December 11, 1994, explosion killed a Japanese passenger and injured ten others.

A month later, Yousef and colleague Abdul Hakim Murad were assembling bombs in a Manila apartment when they accidentally unleashed a smoke cloud, alerting a building security guard. Yousef escaped and traveled directly to Pakistan. Authorities who arrested Murad discovered bomb-making materials and manuals, a map of Manila showing the route Pope John Paul II's entourage would take during an upcoming visit, and a laptop computer showing the flight schedules of the U.S. airlines Yousef intended to blow up. The laptop also contained Yousef's "Manifesto" pledging terrorism to punish Americans for their government's support of Israel.

At long last, the DSS got a big break in the World Trade Center bombing case on February 3, 1995. A nervous-sounding man claiming to have information called the U.S. embassy in Islamabad, Pakistan, at 10:45 A.M. Agent Jeff Riner took the call. Art Maurel was the RSO in charge of all security and counter-terrorism matters at the embassy. The man had seen the U.S. Department of State poster offering a $2 million reward for information that would lead to the arrest of the suspects.

Riner was skeptical. Large cash rewards had helped catch many terrorists, but they also tended to draw con artists, crazies, and crooks. In a few cases, informants had lured agents into traps.

Riner and Agent Bill Miller met the alleged informant at a safe location away from the embassy. "The more I questioned him," Riner said later, "the more excited I got."

Convinced that the man had information only an insider would know, the two agents disguised the nervous man so he wouldn't be recognized and took him back to the U.S. embassy where they interviewed him for four more hours. After further interviews the next day, the DSS team knew the informant was truthful. His knowledge of Yousef included the terrorist's current location, travel itinerary, and activities.

An arrest was imminent. RSO Maurel contacted Washington with the good news. The DSS and the Federal Bureau of Investigation scrambled to send additional agents to Pakistan, but then the informant called Agent Miller on February 6 with good and bad news. Although he had seen Yousef in Islamabad, the bomb-maker was about to depart by bus to Peshawar in northwestern Pakistan and escape into Afghanistan. The agents had to act fast; they had no time to wait for Washington's reinforcements.

The three DSS Agents requested help from the embassy's Drug Enforcement Agency (DEA) office and staked out both the Su Casa guest house where the informant said Yousef was staying and the bus terminal. Maurel called his police and intelligence contacts with the government of Pakistan and let them know the agents' plan. The informant would go into Su Casa and if he encountered Yousef, he would leave and signal the agents by walking halfway across the street, taking his hat off, and brushing his hair back with his hand.

The informant signaled at 9:30 A.M., on February 7.

Riner, a DEA agent, and a team of Pakistani authorities burst into Yousef's room. A Pakistani police officer slammed Yousef against the wall and asked Riner, "Is this your terrorist?"

Riner pulled out a photograph of Yousef and held it to the suspect's head. He studied Yousef's mangled fingers and scarred face. "It's him. Arrest him, please."

The agents discovered explosives and other incriminating evidence in Yousef's room. Clearly, he had been planning other attacks.

In August 1996, DSS agents Mike Posillico and Riner were given secret orders and airline tickets to a foreign country. Their assignment was to give the informant, now in hiding, a check for $2 million. America pays it debts.

* * *

Some of the many other incidents in which DSS agents become embroiled defy the imagination. Training, skill, and sometimes luck have saved agents' lives over the years. For example, a team of terrorists ambushed a three-car motorcade in which U.S. Ambassador John Gunther Dean was riding in Beirut. Agent Robert Morris was in charge of protecting Dean when the gunmen sprayed the partially armored vehicles with bullets from automatic weapons. One terrorist hoisted an American light antitank weapon (LAW) to his shoulder and fired. The rocket hit the pavement near the motorcade, sending shrapnel into two tires of the ambassador's limousine. Agent Morris aimed his M-16 at the ambush team and fired thirty-two rounds on fully automatic, enabling the motorcade's drivers to escape. Investigators later found blood trails at the scene.

Plastic inserts had been installed inside the limousine's tires in case of just such an emergency. The manufacturer guaranteed that the plastic insert would allow the vehicle to be driven at forty miles an hour. "There's no way I was going to crawl out of that ambush at forty miles per hour," one of the drivers told me. We now know they hold at ninety.

Agents Dennis Williams and John Hucke were driving a station wagon in Cairo, Egpyt, on May 26, 1987, when gunmen pulled alongside and peppered the car with AK-47 assault rifles, blowing out the windows. They also tried to force the agents off the road. Williams instantaneously slammed his car into the terrorists' vehicle, quickly maneuvered his station wagon into a U-turn, and escaped. Defensive-driving techniques, skill, and luck saved their lives.

Luck can be a terrific partner. One time in Beirut, I got up at 3:00 A.M. to get a drink of water and returned to a machine gun round that had slammed through the hotel wall and plowed deeply into the middle of my bed. On another occasion, a sniper put a hole through a Lebanese road map that my partner Tony Deibler and I were studying. We assumed the map wasn't the target.

One thing I learned early on about the protection business is that you get a lot of late night calls and can end up in some very wild and wonderful places—and sometimes just wild.

"Did I wake you?" asked the voice on the phone long before dawn.

Too tired to retort, I replied, "Of course you woke me, it's three-thirty in the morning!"

"Guess where you're going?" the man asked. I was groggy, the telephone had just awakened me, my girlfriend, and my golden retriever, and the character on the other end wanted to play guessing games.

"Where am I going, damn it!" I shouted, startling the dog.

"You and Frank Provyn are going to the Okefenokee Swamp," the DSS Command Center agent responded, suddenly sounding professional.

"Why are we going there?" I asked, genuinely puzzled.

"Can't tell you until you get here."

If I were going to be spending time in the snake- and alligator-infested Okefenokee Swamp, I was glad Frank Provyn was going to be my partner. He was a former U.S. Army Ranger and a sniper in Vietnam, and I knew from past experience that he didn't whine when the situation got tense and uncomfortable. Like me, Frank was more comfortable with a backpack than a briefcase, and preferred camouflage fatigues to a Brooks Brothers suit.

Frank called next. "Did we piss somebody off?"

"Haven't we always," I replied.

We learned that we would be protecting a VIP, who must remain anonymous, who had been given permission to canoe and hike the Okefenokee Swamp from Georgia to Florida. Despite a recent attempt on his life and being dogged by a foreign terrorist group, the VIP refused to cancel the adventure he had been planning for an entire year.

Frank and I respected the man for not allowing a gang of thugs to control his life, but I gave the protectee my honest assessment of the situation. "It's a lot easier to have a man killed in the swamp than it is to protect him."

I also told him that if we were attacked by a gang of snakes, alligators, or other creeping critters, he was on his own. He thought I was kidding.

"How important is this guy?" I asked Frank. While I was putting our weapons and camping gear together, Frank had been in touch with the White House and the "seventh floor" at the State Department, where the Secretary of State resides.

"Let me put it bluntly," Frank explained. "If anything happens to our protectee, there better be two dead agents."

I immediately requested that the DSS assign Agents Rick Watts and Bill Elderbaum to our team to even up the odds a bit. Rick and I had served together in Bogotá, Beirut, and San Salvador. Elderbaum and I had known each other in Vietnam and he had been a Prince Georges County, Maryland, police officer. I knew that Watts and Elderbaum were capable of controlled yet extremely explosive violence, important qualities in a fire fight.

My request was denied. Our protectee had insisted on no more than two agents. "Too many agents will ruin my trip. Besides, there are rules on how many people are allowed into the swamp at any one time."

I pointed out that the hit team could ruin the trip, too, and that I doubted they would adhere to the rules.

Ten hours later the three of us, Frank, the protectee and I, were in the Okefenokee Swamp, paddling two canoes through a majestic vine-covered canal. We saw five snakes within the first ten minutes. Within twenty minutes we saw our first alligator, six feet from our canoe. Five minutes after that we had to make an important decision: who was going to get out of the canoe and wade over to some fallen trees that were blocking our path. We flipped a coin. Frank lost.

That night, and every night that week, our protectee slept soundly under mosquito netting on an air mattress while Frank and I unrolled our sleeping bags on the hard, damp earth. Frank would sleep for two hours while I stood guard, and then I traded places with him. An exhausting arrangement after paddling in the hot sun all day.

On the third night Frank woke me. "We've got company," he said in a hushed voice. I grabbed a pump shotgun and Frank already had an Uzi in his hands. Had I a choice, I was hoping it was the terrorists and not a gang of alligators.

Suddenly two deer crashed loudly through our camp almost trampling our protectee, who slept through the ambush.

"If that happens again we're going to have venison for breakfast," said Frank.

The next day, while paddling through a narrow canal, Frank and I pondered heavy philosophical questions. "Do you think we can charge for hotel rooms on our vouchers?" "Aren't you glad we're getting $36.00 per day for meals?"

We counted sixty-four snakes and seventeen alligators on our trip, but no terrorists.

The trip ended and I delivered our protectee directly to the White House where he was staying.

"I can arrange for you to spend the night at the White House if you like," the protectee offered, not realizing that he didn't have the authority. I think he was a bit surprised when I politely declined the offer.

Too many politicians hang around the White House. Besides, I was anxious to get back to my girlfriend and my golden retriever.

Epilogue

R AMZI YOUSEF, THE ALLEGED MASTERMIND OF THE 1993 World Trade Center bombing, confessed that he had hoped to kill 250,000 civilians in an attempt to persuade the United States to stop supporting Israel. He sought destruction on the scale of the bomb dropped on Hiroshima in 1945.

We live in an age of unimaginable rage and apocalyptic arsenals: nuclear, chemical, and biological. We live at a time when social, political, and religious "causes" greatly outnumber the cures. And if terrorists have demonstrated anything in recent years, it is that they are willing and capable of taking advantage of these conditions to inflict mass casualties, change targets, and develop new techniques and strategies to defeat our security.

Intelligence indicators strongly suggest that a wide range of foreign and domestic terrorist groups, including more than 400 right-wing hate and militia-type organizations, will increasingly operate in the United States. There is no doubt that these groups will commit assassinations, kidnappings, robberies, and sabotage to promote their diverse causes, utilizing vehicle bombs, double bombs, and rampage shootings to punctuate their demands. Future terrorist operations in the United States will almost certainly include suicide missions and simultaneous attacks on "soft" unprotected targets such as skyscrapers, subways, and stadiums.

Bombs concealed in books, briefcases, boxes, and suitcases will continue to be smuggled into airports, government buildings, and businesses. Booby-trapped devices hidden in baby carriages, flower arrangements, fire extinguishers, computers, and cassette recorders will detonate in hotels, embassies, and private residences. These are not predictions—they are promises.

Assassins will do as they have always done. Some will suddenly emerge from a crowd and start shooting, and others, preferring the sniper's role, will stand a long way off and slowly squeeze the trigger. During the next decade, political assassins in the United States will pose as police officers, postal employees, photographers, plumbers, pilots, priests, and members of the press. Extremists will use the "unwitting accomplice" tactic whereby innocent people are duped into delivering bombs, or will magically pull firearms from folded newspapers, ankle holsters, flight bags, camera cases, or slings on fake broken arms. Some male terrorists will disguise themselves as women, and female operatives will take advantage of their gender to defeat our security over and over again.

Like stage magicians, many terrorists will rely on props to create an illusion to deceive the public. A terrorist entering a synagogue could don a yarmulke. If the target is a church or someone attending a church service, the assassin might wear a crucifix or carry a prayer book. Worldwide, there have been twenty-two documented cases in which terrorists hollowed out copies of the Bible or the Koran in order to conceal bombs or guns.

When the target is a hospital or one of its patients, terrorists may steal white coats, put stethoscopes around their necks, and, abracadabra, transform themselves into doctors and nurses. Subtle forms of deception will also be used by terrorists conducting surveillance. They will pretend to be joggers, vendors, beggars, and lovers on a bench. Operatives surveilling American interests will walk dogs around military installations, stand at bus stops and pay telephones in front of government buildings, and take photographs of potential targets while posing as tourists.

In the coming years, agents of chaos and mass destruction in the United States could just as easily be a taxi or delivery driver, a well-dressed elderly couple, a pregnant woman, or an invalid in a wheelchair. Utilizing a repertoire of disguises and diversions, ploys and props, false stories and false identifications, today's terrorists are truly masters of deception.

Terrorism, the new warfare, is here to stay. To defeat the enemy, the public will have to strive for higher levels of co-operation with the police and develop an educated eye for deception. Underestimating the terrorist threat in the United States would be a tragic mistake.

APPENDIX

A Chronicle of Terrorism in the United States

BETWEEN JANUARY 1, 1977, AND JANUARY 1, 1998, I recorded 3,150 incidents of political violence in the United States perpetrated by at least 128 domestic and international terrorist groups. These incidents included murder and attempted murder, bombings, kidnappings, hijackings, sabotage, prison escapes, arson, attacks on police, building takeovers, hostage-taking situations, and robberies of banks, armored cars, gun stores, and explosives storage sites. The following is a sampling of these incidents.

January 14, 1980, Wisconsin. Several members of the Armed Forces of National Liberation (FALN) raided a National Guard Armory in hopes of stealing antitank rockets, mortars, M-60 machine guns, and M-16 automatic shoulder weapons.

January 22, 1980, California. A bomb exploded at Los Angeles International Airport in the luggage area used by China Airlines, causing $25,000 in damages. The Los Angeles residence of a son of General Wang Sheng of Taiwan was bombed March 10, 1980, but he escaped injury. On July 28, 1980, a booby-trapped bomb delivered to a private residence in Los

Angeles killed the brother-in-law of the mayor of Kaohsiung, Taiwan. Although no group claimed credit for the bombings, analysts and investigators believe the Taiwanese Independence Movement (TIM) was responsible for all three attacks. TIM was probably also responsible for a bombing in College Park, Maryland, on June 27, 1981, that killed a scholar from the People's Republic of China and wounded four others. On October 15, 1984, in Dale City, California, Henry Liu, a Chinese American author and critic of the Taiwan regime, was assassinated at the behest of the Taiwan intelligence service. This latter incident is an example of state-directed terrorism.

April 4, 1980, Illinois. Police in Evanston arrested eleven members of the Armed Forces of National Liberation (FALN) who had assembled for the purpose of robbing an armored truck. Authorities seized a stolen truck, several stolen vans and cars, assorted weapons, and various disguises and articles of false identification. The arrests by street police officers certainly prevented many future murders, bombings, and robberies.

June 3, 1980, Washington, D.C. A powerful bomb planted by the Croatian Freedom Fighters (CFF) exploded at the home of the chargé d'affaires of the Yugoslavian embassy. The blast caused extensive damage to the home and broke windows in neighboring houses. From 1976 to 1982 Croatian extremists committed sixty-seven acts of political violence in the United States including eleven assassinations and attempted assassinations, hijackings, consulate takeovers, mail bombings and bombings of court rooms, banks, restaurants, airline offices and the Statue of Liberty. Proindependence Croatian terrorist groups such as the CFF, Optor, and the Croatian Nationalist Army, operated primarily in California, Connecticut, Illinois, New York, Pennsylvania, and Wisconsin.

July 17, 1980, California. A mail bomb delivered to the offices of ProWest Computer Corporation in Manhattan Beach,

California, killed Patricia Wilkerson, a thirty-two-year-old secretary and mother of two. On February 7, 1994, Robert Manning, a member of the Jewish Defense League (JDL) was convicted of the murder and sentenced to life in prison.

July 22, 1980, Maryland. An American member of the Islamic Guerrillas of America (IGA) donned a postal uniform and assassinated Ali Akbar Tabatabai at his Bethesda, Maryland, home. Tabatabai was an outspoken critic of Khomeini's Revolutionary Government of Iran and founder of the anti-Khomeini Iran Freedom Foundation.

September 11, 1980, New York. Omega-7 gunmen assassinated Felix Garcia-Rodriguez, an attaché to the Cuban Mission at the United Nations, on a busy New York street. Omega-7 is an anti-Castro Cuban exile group responsible for scores of bombings and assassinations in the United States and other countries.

October 12, 1980, New York and California. The Justice Commandos of the Armenian Genocide (JCAG) claimed responsibility for simultaneous bombings in Los Angeles and New York City. Six sticks of dynamite hidden in a car detonated in front of the Turkish Mission to the United Nations in New York, injuring six people. In Los Angeles, a passerby was injured when a bomb exploded at a travel agency owned by a man of Turkish descent. Armenian terrorists have been responsible for more than two dozen violent incidents in the United States, including four assassinations and bombings of consulates, convention centers, banks, and private residences and businesses.

October 14, 1980, Colorado. Eugene Tafoya, a former Green Beret and Vietnam veteran recruited by Colonel Qaddafi of Libya, attempted to assassinate Faisal Zagallai, a thirty-five-year-old Libyan graduate student attending Colorado State University. Zagallai survived the attack, which occurred in his apartment, but one bullet passed through his skull and left him blind in one eye. A second bullet entered his right temple and remains lodged in his palate.

April 16, 1981, New York. Two police officers sitting in a patrol car were gravely wounded by two Black Liberation Army terrorists who leaped out of a van the officers had stopped. The gunmen fired thirty shots from 9-millimeter fifteen-shot automatic handguns. Officer John G. Scarangella, forty-two, was wounded in the jaw, the right ear, and a leg. His partner, Richard Rainey, thirty-four, was shot fourteen times in the legs and back. After firing through the windshield, the gunmen came around to the sides of the patrol car and emptied their guns at the officers inside.

May 16, 1981, New York. A nineteen-year-old news vendor was killed by a booby-trapped briefcase that was left in a restroom at John F. Kennedy International Airport. Two other bombs, one in a congested terminal area and another in a woman's restroom, were also discovered at the airport and diffused. The bombs were planted by the Puerto Rican terrorist group FALN.

October 20, 1981, New York. Members of five domestic terrorist organizations attacked and robbed a Brink's armored car at the Nanuet Mall. The terrorists killed a Brink's guard and two policemen and fled with $1,589,000 in cash.

December 21, 1981, New Jersey. Philip Lamonaco, a New Jersey State Trooper, was murdered by two members of the Sam Melville–Jonathan Jackson Brigade (SMJJB) during a routine traffic stop. The SMJJB is an "anti-imperialist" American terrorist group responsible for several bombings and bank robberies. Members of the group would later refer to themselves as the United Freedom Front (UFF). Member Thomas Manning was convicted of the murder on January 18, 1987, and sentenced to life imprisonment.

January 28, 1982, California. The Turkish consul general to Los Angeles, Kemal Arikan, was assassinated by two gunmen who approached his car from separate directions and opened fire. The attack was claimed by the Justice Commandos of the Armenian Genocide (JCAG).

February 7, 1982, Massachusetts. A Massachusetts state trooper, making a routine traffic stop, noticed that one of the two male occupants of the car was wearing a bulletproof vest. While the officer was waiting for other officers to arrive at the scene, a shootout occurred. One of the motorists escaped and the other was captured. The two men were members of the Sam Melville–Jonathan Jackson Brigade and the United Freedom Front.

February 19, 1982, Washington, D.C. The Aeroflot Soviet Airlines office was damaged by a Jewish Defense League (JDL) pipe bomb.

April 5, 1982, New York. An elderly woman was killed and eight people were injured in a fire caused by a firebomb at the Lebanese-owned Tripoli Restaurant in Brooklyn. In claiming credit, a spokesman for the JDL stated, "This should serve notice that Jewish blood is not cheap."

April 28, 1982, New York. A pipe bomb placed by the JDL exploded in the revolving glass door at Lufthansa German Airlines on Fifth Avenue.

May 4, 1982, Massachusetts. Orhan Gunduz, the honorary Turkish consul to Boston, was assassinated as his vehicle slowed in heavy traffic. The gunman, who was wearing a jogging outfit, fired thirteen rounds from a 9-millimeter handgun, hitting Gunduz nine times. The brazen attack, claimed by the Justice Commandos of the Armenian Genocide, occurred just 150 feet from the Somerville police station.

May 31, 1982, California. Three Armenian terrorists attempted to bomb the Air Canada freight terminal at Los Angeles International Airport. The Los Angeles Police Department bomb squad deactivated the device fifteen minutes before detonation. The terrorists were retaliating against Canadian targets because Toronto police arrested four members of the Armenian Secret Army for the Liberation of Armenia (ASALA) on May 18, 1982.

August 11, 1982, Hawaii. A bomb, placed beneath a passenger's seat, exploded aboard a Pan Am jumbo jet about to land in Honolulu following a flight from Tokyo's Narita Airport. One sixteen-year-old Japanese passenger was killed and fourteen others were wounded. The bomb caused the plane to lose altitude but the crew recovered and landed safely in Honolulu. The May 15 Arab Organization is believed to be responsible for the bombing.

September 20, 1982, New York. A bomb caused extensive damage to Bankers Trust and to buildings across the street on Park Avenue. A man with a Spanish accent who claimed to be with the Armed Forces of National Liberation (FALN) stated, "We have just bombed a mid-town bank to protest the United States support of the Israeli massacre of Palestinian people."

December 16, 1982, New York. The United Freedom Front (UFF) detonated bombs at the IBM Building in Harrison and the South African Purchasing Office in Elmont. Between December 16, 1982 and February 23, 1985, a series of eighteen bombings in New York and Washington, D.C., were claimed by the UFF, Revolutionary Fighting Group (RFG), Armed Resistance Unit (ARU), and the Red Guerrilla Resistance (RGR). The targets bombed by these groups included the U.S. Capitol building, the National War College, Motorola Corporation, Israeli Aircraft Industries, General Electric, Union Carbide and seven U.S. military facilities. All available evidence indicates that these were not separate groups, but one left-wing group, the UFF, that used a variety of names. Some UFF members were involved in an earlier terrorist group, the Sam Melville–Jonathan Jackson Brigade.

December 31, 1982, New York. The FALN planted bombs at four government buildings on New Year's Eve, seriously injuring three police officers. Patrolman Rocco Pascarella had a leg amputated following an explosion at police headquarters. Detective Salvatore Pastorella, assigned to the bomb squad, lost the fingers of his right hand and suffered extensive damage to his eyes and ears while removing a bomb from the Metropolitan Correctional Center. His partner, Detective Anthony Senft, received injuries to his face and right eye.

February 13, 1983, North Dakota. A shootout occurred at a roadblock in Medina when carloads of U.S. marshals, sheriffs, and police stopped members of the Posse Comitatus and tried to arrest Gordon W. Kahl. Posse Comitatus is an anti-Semitic, antitax group that believes there is no legitimate form of government beyond the county level. U.S. Marshal Kenneth Muir and Deputy Marshal Robert Cheshire were killed in the shootout. Three other lawmen and Kahl's twenty-year-old son were wounded. Kahl, a decorated and twice-wounded World War II veteran, drove his wounded son to the hospital where the wounded marshals were also being treated, and became a fugitive. To the survivalist right, Kahl became an overnight hero; he had won an all-out gun battle with forces of the so-called "Zionist Occupational Government" (ZOG). The term "ZOG" is used by racists and neo-Nazis to reflect their belief that the federal government and the U.S. banking system are controlled by Jews for their own benefit. On June 3, 1983, in Imboden, Arkansas, nearly 100 law enforcement officers assaulted a bunkerlike farmhouse where Kahl and more than 100,000 rounds of ammunition were holed up. When the fierce firefight ended, Sheriff Gene Matthews and Gordon Kahl were dead. Kahl, a Posse patriarch, is considered a martyr by right-wing extremists.

April 27, 1983, Florida.   Three package bombs were mailed to three Haitian government officials and one Haitian businessman at four separate locations. The bombs were all discovered and defused.

September 12, 1983, Connecticut.   Victor Gerena, a guard for Wells Fargo armored car service and a member of a pro-independence Puerto Rican terrorist group called the Macheteros, who blew up thirteen U.S. military jet fighters in San Juan on January 12, 1981, robbed a Wells Fargo warehouse of slightly more than seven million dollars in cash. Gerena is currently living in Cuba.

June 18, 1984, Colorado.   A neo-Nazi group called The Order, assassinated Alan Berg, a controversial Jewish talk-show host. Berg, who denounced right-wing terrorist groups, was mowed down with twelve slugs from an illegal Ingram MAC 10 automatic as he stepped out of his car in front of his Denver home. The Order also attacked a Brink's armored vehicle outside Ukiah, California, in 1984 and stole a staggering $3.6 million, which was used to finance additional right-wing activities. In 1985, twenty-four members of the group were sentenced to prison terms. The arrests and convictions halted a series of planned assassinations.

June 30, 1984, Arkansas.   White supremacist, Richard Wayne Snell, an Oklahoma survivalist and member of the Covenant, Sword, and Arm of the Lord (CSA), murdered Louis Bryant, thirty-seven, a black Arkansas state police trooper, who had stopped him for a minor traffic violation. Convicted of killing Trooper Bryant and a pawnshop owner he thought was Jewish, Snell was executed on April 19, 1995, the same day Timothy McVeigh blew up the Alfred P. Murrah Federal Building in Oklahoma City. April 19 is an extremely important anniversary date for right-wing groups in the United States. On April 19, 1993, federal authorities raided the Branch Davidian compound in Waco, Texas, culminating in the fiery death of seventy-five Davidians, including many children. In Lexington, Massachusetts, on April 19, 1775, British "redcoats" attempted to destroy weapons stockpiled by the colonists and to arrest John Hancock and Samuel Adams. But on Lexington Green the Minutemen, colonial militiamen, fought back. "The shot heard around the world" galvanized militia patriots in the thirteen colonies and launched the American Revolution. Today, many right-wing militias want to declare April 19 as "the right to bear arms day."

November 29, 1984, New Jersey. Susan Lisa Rosenberg and Timothy A. Blunk, members of the May 19 Communist Organization (M19CO), were arrested by local police officers as they loaded an Uzi submachine gun, a shotgun, and 672 pounds of explosives into a rented storage locker. Rosenberg had been a federal fugitive since 1982 for alleged participation in the 1979 prison escape of Black Liberation Army member, Joanne Chesimard, and for the October 20, 1981, Brink's robbery and slayings in Nanuet, New York. Blunk was wanted for being an accessory in the Brinks attack and for a September 2, 1984, robbery of a Stop and Shop Supermarket in Cromwell, Connecticut. The 672 pounds of explosives had been stolen in Austin, Texas, in 1980. The M19CO is a Marxist–Leninist group that openly advocates the overthrow of the U.S. government through armed struggle and the use of violence.

April 15, 1985, Missouri. David C. Tate, a neo-Nazi and member of The Order, opened fire on two Missouri highway patrolmen who had stopped his van for a routine traffic inspection. Trooper Jimmie L. Linegar, thirty-one, the father of two small children, was killed and Trooper Allen Hines, thirty-six, was wounded in the shoulder, arm, and hip. When Tate was stopped, he was en route to a right-wing Covenant, Sword and Arm of the Lord compound located along the Missouri–Arkansas border, and his van was packed with weapons and explosives. Tate, twenty-two, was captured April 20, 1985, in Forsyth, Missouri, and is now serving a life sentence. Since most members of The Order are tax-protestors, the date of this incident, income tax deadline day, may be significant. The Order is an offshoot of the Aryan Nations (AN), is fighting the Zionist Occupation Government, and fosters a hatred for the federal government, especially law enforcement agencies.

May 4, 1985, Pennsylvania. Five Sikh extremists, including one U.S. citizen, were arrested by the FBI after an undercover operation revealed they were seeking weapons and explosives and were planning to assassinate Prime Minister Rajiv Gandhi when he visited the United States. From June 1984 to May 1986, Sikh extremists were responsible for at least fourteen terrorist incidents in six states, including murders and bombings. On June 17, 1984, Sikh extremists bombed the Vendanta Society (an Indian cultural organization) in Seattle, Washington. The Vendanta Society in Kansas City, Missouri, was bombed June 20, 1984. On August 1, 1984, Sikhs kidnapped and murdered a prominent Indian physician in Missouri. On the same day, an Indian government official was shot to death, along with his wife and a relative in Tacoma, Washington. On May 30, 1986, five Sikh terrorists who were planning to place a bomb in an Air India aircraft at New York's John F. Kennedy International Airport, were arrested by Canadian authorities in Canada. Sikh terrorists want to carve out an independent Sikh state called Khalistan (Land of the Pure) from Indian territory.

August 15, 1985, New Jersey. Tscherim Soobzokov, an American citizen, who had been a member of the Nazi Waffen SS, was awakened by a neighbor at his home in Paterson and told that his car was on fire. Rushing outside, Soobzokov tripped a booby-trapped pipe bomb, allegedly planted by the Jewish Defense League, killing himself and wounding the innocent neighbor. Soobzokov, sixty-one, had been accused of falsifying his wartime activities in order to enter the United States in 1955, but all charges had been dropped when he showed the court he had indeed disclosed his Waffen SS membership. He had worked for the CIA in the Middle East before moving to America.

August 16, 1985, Massachusetts.   A bomb at the Boston offices of the American-Arab Anti-Discrimination Committee (ADC), blew up in the faces of two bomb disposal experts. Officer Randolph LaMattina, forty, was placing the bomb into a special trailer when the device exploded, causing extensive damage to both hands. His partner, Michael Boccuzzi, fifty-seven, was knocked down by the force of the blast and hospitalized with chest pains. The ADC had received numerous threats from the Jewish Defense League.

September 6, 1985, New York.   Elmars Sprogis, a sixty-nine-year-old former Latvian policeman, was slightly injured when a pipe bomb placed on his front steps exploded. Sprogis, a retired construction worker, had recently been cleared on charges that he helped kill Jews during World War II. An innocent bystander, Robert Seifried, had both his legs blown off. Seifried, who was not acquainted with Sprogis, had been trying to put out a fire on Sprogis's porch, when the bomb exploded. The fire had been set to lure Sprogis out of his home. The Jewish Defense League claimed responsibility for the attack.

October 11, 1985, California.   Alex M. Odeh, the West Coast director of the American-Arab Anti-Discrimination Committee (ADC), was killed when a bomb detonated in his office. The explosion injured seven other people in adjoining offices. As Odeh unlocked his office and stepped inside, a trip wire attached to the door set off a powerful bomb that tore through the lower half of his body. In a television interview the night before he was killed, Odeh said it was time for the American people to "understand the Palestinian side of the story." The bomb that killed Odeh was similar to devices the Jewish Defense League had used in the past.

September 15, 1986, Idaho. A pipe bomb exploded at the Coeur d'Alene residence of Father William Wassmuth, a Catholic priest. On September 29, 1986, additional bombs were planted at the Federal Building housing FBI offices, an Armed Forces Recruiting Station, and two commercial establishments. No group claimed responsibility for the bombings but the FBI believes all five devices were the work of individuals affiliated with the Aryan Nations (AN). The AN, which has a twenty-acre compound near Hayden Lake, Idaho, advocates the elimination of Jews, blacks, and other nonwhites from society.

March 2, 1987, California. Four explosive devices detonated near the Federal Building at Laguna Niguel. The Federal Building houses several Internal Revenue Service (IRS) offices. A fifth device, which did not detonate, was recovered on the roof of the building.

April 19, 1987, Montana. A bomb detonated beneath a police vehicle at the Missoula Police Department. A member of the Aryan Nations (AN) called police and claimed responsibility for the attack. The caller ended his conversation by saying "Heil Hitler!"

December 14, 1987, California. Armenian terrorist Vicken Tcharkhutian, the chief bomb-maker for the Armenian Secret Army for the Liberation of Armenia (ASALA), was sentenced to twelve years' imprisonment for his role in two bombings and two attempted bombings in Los Angeles. The bombing targets were the Air Canada office at Los Angeles International Airport, a Carpeteria store, a Swiss bank, and the Swiss Consulate.

April 12, 1988, New Jersey. Japanese Red Army (JRA) member, Yu Kikumura, was arrested for suspicious behavior at a rest stop along the New Jersey Turnpike. Inside Kikumura's car, police found three homemade antipersonnel bombs that were intended for a terrorist operation in the United States to coincide with the second anniversary of the U.S. retaliatory airstrike on Libya. On February 8, 1989, Kikumura was sentenced to thirty years' imprisonment for bomb possession with the intent to kill. (On May 30, 1972, three JRA members attacked Tel Aviv's Lod International Airport killing twenty-eight people and wounding seventy-eight.)

March 10, 1989, California. A pipe bomb exploded beneath a van owned by Sharon L. Rogers, the wife of U.S. Navy Captain Will C. Rogers III, the commander of USS *Vincennes*. Mrs. Rogers escaped unharmed prior to detonation. Authorities believe the bombing was related to the July 3, 1988, incident in which the USS *Vincennes* shot down Iran Air flight 565, killing 290 civilians.

April 3, 1989, Arizona. The Animal Liberation Front (ALF) claimed responsibility for two fires at the University of Arizona causing approximately $100,000 damage and the theft of more than 1,000 research animals. The two buildings targeted were the Pharmacy Microbiology Building and the Office for the Division of Animal Resources. On July 4, 1989, in Lubbock, Texas, ALF operatives broke into the Health Sciences Center at Texas Tech University, destroyed sophisticated machinery, released research animals, and stole research documents.

August 19, 1989, California. Doan Van Toai, the executive directory of the Institute for Democracy in Vietnam (IDV), was shot several times by two unidentified Asians in Fresno. Toai is a well-known Vietnamese writer and political activist and has received several threats on his life, including a bullet in the mail. Many in the Vietnamese community believe that he is a supporter of the Socialist Republic of Vietnam. No group claimed responsibility for the attempted assassination, but the

Vietnamese Organization to Exterminate Communism and Restore the Nation (VOECRN) has claimed credit for other terrorist incidents, including murder.

February 17, 1990, California.   The FBI arrested an individual who allegedly had been hired to commit two assassinations on behalf of a foreign country. The plot was instituted and directed by a diplomat assigned to an embassy in the United States. The alleged assassin was subsequently released from custody and fled the United States before he could be brought to trial. The diplomat was expelled from the United States. This case is an example of terrorism that is invisible to the public.

September 7, 1990, Washington, D.C.   Three female members of the May 19 Communist Organization (M19CO)—Marilyn Jean Buck, Laura Jane Whitehorn, and Linda Sue Evans —pled guilty to charges relating to the 1983 bombing of the U.S. Capitol and several other targets in the Washington, D.C., area. The M19CO is a Marxist–Leninist terrorist organization that openly advocates the overthrow of the U.S. government through armed struggle and the use of violence.

November 5, 1990, New York.   Rabbi Meir Kahane, fifty-eight, controversial leader of the Jewish Defense League, was shot and killed while speaking to a group of supporters at the Marriott East Side Hotel. Egyptian-born El Sayyid A. Nosair, the alleged gunman, reportedly walked up to Kahane as he was answering questions and shot him in the head and chest with a .357 Magnum revolver. Nosair, a naturalized American citizen, ran from the hotel, commandeered a taxi, and engaged in a gun battle with a uniformed U.S. Postal Service Officer. The officer was wounded in the arm and Nosair was hit in the stomach and captured.

January 23, 1993, Virginia.   Mir Aimal Kansi, a twenty-eight-year-old Pakistani, opened fire on motorists who were stopped at a red light in front of CIA headquarters in Langley. In a matter of seconds Frank Darling, twenty-eight, and Lansing Bennett, sixty-six, both CIA employees, were killed, and three other CIA employees were permanently injured. Kansi allegedly told a roommate that he was angry about the treatment of Muslims in Bosnia and that he was going to get even by shooting up the CIA, the White House, or the Israeli Embassy.

February 26, 1993, New York. A group of Middle Eastern terrorists loaded 1,200 pounds of explosives into a rented van and drove the vehicle to a parking garage beneath the World Trade Center in New York City. The powerful bomb killed six people, injured more than 1,000, and caused more than a half billion dollars damage. Ramzi Yousef, one of the terrorists, said he intended for the bomb to topple the two 110-story towers in hopes of causing 250,000 casualties. The stated purpose for the bombing was to persuade the United States to stop supporting Israel.

October 6, 1993, Massachusetts. Radical fugitive Katherine Ann Power was sentenced to eight to twelve years in prison for her participation in the September 23, 1970, robbery of State Street Bank and Trust and the murder of Boston Patrolman Walter Schroeder. Power and Susan Saxe, both Brandeis University students in 1970, robbed the bank along with three career criminals in order to raise money for their "revolution." The three career criminals had been studying at Brandeis under an inmate tutoring program. Responding to a silent alarm, Office Schroeder approached the front of the bank where he was shot in the back by William "Lefty" Gilday. Power had been a fugitive for twenty-three years before surrendering to authorities in September 1993.

December 10, 1993, Virginia. William W. Graham, thirty-nine, a self-described revolutionary, was sentenced to life in prison for a 1972 bank robbery in Crystal City, Virginia. Israel

Gonzalez, a twenty-seven-year-old Arlington police officer, and Harry J. Candee, the bank manager, were killed during the holdup. On the morning of the robbery, Graham and three accomplices severed the bank's phone and alarm wires. Then, posing as telephone company employees and using a stolen C&P Telephone Co. van, the four terrorists entered the bank under the guise of being repairmen. The group then shot Candee in the head and bludgeoned a female bank teller. Officer Gonzales, who was summoned from the street by an employee, shot one of the robbers twice before being shot six times by the terrorists. Five days later (October 28, 1972) the four men shot an Eastern Airlines ticket agent to death and hijacked a jetliner from Houston Intercontinental Airport, forcing the pilot to fly to Cuba.

March 1, 1994, New York. A twenty-eight-year-old Lebanese cabdriver opened fire on a van load of Hasidic students crossing the Brooklyn Bridge, killing one and wounding three others. A Manhattan jury found Rashid Baz guilty of murder and attempted murder on December 1, 1994. Baz was reportedly seeking revenge for the massacre that occurred in Hebron on February 25, 1994. In that incident Baruch Goldstein, a New York-born Israeli settler opened fire during prayers at the Tomb of the Patriarchs, killing thirty Moslem worshipers.

March 9, 1994, Florida. Daniel Buron, an outspoken opponent of Haiti's military dictatorship, was gunned down by two men on a Miami street following a meeting with the Veye Yo political group. Veye Yo means "Beware of Them" in Creole, the popular language of Haiti. Buron became the fourth supporter of then-deposed Haitian President Jean-Bertrand Aristide to be assassinated in Miami since 1991.

October 21, 1994, Missouri. Three members of the Abu Nidal Organization (ANO), which has been described as the most dangerous terrorist group in the world, were sentenced to twenty-one months in prison for plotting terrorism in the United States. The three men had plotted to kill Jews, blow up the Israeli Embassy in Washington, D.C., and kill anyone who exposed the plots. Charges against a fourth defendant, Zein Isa, sixty-three, were dropped because he was already on Missouri's death row for murdering his daughter at the family's apartment in 1989. She was killed because the conspirators feared she would expose their plots. Believing that Zein Isa was involved in terrorist activities, the FBI had bugged his apartment and caught the young girl's death on tape. On the chilling recording Isa shouted in Arabic, "Die! Die quickly! Die, my daughter, die!", as he stabbed her to death.

March 9, 1995, Pennsylvania. Claude Daniel Marks, forty-five, and Donna Jean Willmott, forty-four, two former members of the radical Weather Underground Organization, were sentenced to prison for plotting to blast FALN leader Oscar Lopez out of Leavenworth Federal Penitentiary. The plot called for landing a helicopter at the prison, detonating explosives, and shooting guards. Marks and Willmott had been living under false names in Squirrel Hill, Pennsylvania, when they were arrested.

April 19, 1995, Oklahoma. Timothy J. McVeigh, a decorated Persian Gulf War veteran, allegedly loaded a Ryder rental truck with 4,000 pounds of explosives and parked the vehicle next to the nine-story Alfred P. Murrah Federal Building in Oklahoma City. The explosion killed 168 people, injured more than 500, disemboweled the federal building, and destroyed or damaged 312 surrounding offices, stores, and apartments.

October 1, 1995, New York. Sheik Omar Abdul Rahman and nine other militant Muslims were convicted of conspiring to carry out a terrorist campaign of bombings and assassinations designed to destroy New York landmarks and kill hundreds of people. In what was meant to be a cataclysmic day of terror, the group had planned to blow up five targets in New York: United Nations headquarters, the Lincoln and Holland tunnels, the George Washington Bridge, and 26 Federal Plaza, the government's main office building in New York.

October 9, 1995, Arizona. Sabotage of a railroad track in a remote area of Hyder, Arizona, caused the derailment of an Amtrak train. One crew member was killed and 78 crew and passengers were injured when four cars of the train carrying 268 people plunged into a thirty-foot-deep ravine. Investigators found a note near the wreckage taking responsibility for the sabotage in the name of Sons of Gestapo and condemning the behavior of federal officers at the assault on the Branch Davidian compound in Waco, Texas, in 1993. The note also mentioned the siege of a white separatist's cabin at Ruby Ridge, Idaho, in 1992. Although the incident appears to be political in nature, investigators are open to the possibility that the derailment was perpetrated by someone with a grudge against railroads.

June 3, 1996, New York. A man charged in Peru with being a member of the Shining Path leftist terrorist organization was arrested in New York. Peruvian officials claim that Julian Salazar Calero, forty-six, participated in numerous attacks that resulted in deaths to police officers and civilians.

July 27, 1996, Georgia. A bomb planted at Centennial Olympic Park during the Atlanta Summer Olympics killed a woman, caused the fatal heart attack of a Turkish cameraman, and injured 111 people. Richard Jewell, thirty-three, a security guard at the Olympics, was initially hailed as a hero for discovering the bomb in a green knapsack and helping to clear people away before it detonated. His actions certainly saved lives, but three days later, Jewell's name was leaked as a prime suspect. After controlling Jewell's life and besmirching his reputation for three months, the authorities and the media finally admitted they had accused the wrong man. Jewell was exonerated of all accusations.

January 16, 1997, Georgia. At 9:30 A.M. a bomb detonated at an Atlanta abortion clinic called the Atlanta Northside Family Planning Services. The explosion shattered glass, brought down parts of walls and ceilings, and caused a small fire. At 10:30 A.M., as police, firefighters, and television news crews assembled at the scene, a second bomb exploded, injuring six people. In a letter claiming responsibility for the double bombing, the Army of God stated that the second bomb, "was aimed at the agents of the so-called federal government, i.e., ATF, FBI, marshals, etc. We declared and will wage total war." The letter stated that the abortion clinic was the target of the first bomb. "The murder of 3.5 million children will not be tolerated."

February 13, 1997, Florida. Hours before Shimon Peres, the former prime minister of Israel, was to speak at the Jacksonville Jewish Center, police received a warning that a bomb had been placed in the synagogue by the so-called American Friends of Islamic Jihad. Police searched the synagogue but did not locate the device. Nine days after the speech, children attending a bat mitzvah at the synagogue discovered the bomb. But the bomb had not been placed by Muslim extremists; it had been planted by a thirty-one-year-old Orthodox Jew. Shimon Peres, a winner of the Nobel Peace Prize, has long been unpopular with right-wing Jews for his role in opening up negotiations with the Palestinians.

February 21, 1997, Georgia. A powerful bomb exploded at The Otherside Lounge, a nightclub popular with gay men and lesbians, injuring four patrons. Police discovered and defused a second bomb that had been placed in the club's parking lot. These bombs were strikingly similar to the bombs used against a suburban abortion clinic on January 16, 1997, and had many of the same characteristics as the Atlanta Centennial Park bombing during the 1996 summer Olympics. The Army of God claimed responsibility for the abortion clinic bombs. In 1994, an anti-abortion activist, believed to be affiliated with the Army of God, shot and killed an abortion doctor and his bodyguard in Pensacola, Florida.

February 23, 1997, New York.   Ali Hassan Abu Kamal, an unstable sixty-nine-year-old Palestinian teacher, opened fire on the observation deck of the Empire State Building, killing one tourist and seriously wounding six others. He then committed suicide. The deranged gunman sought revenge for the treatment of Palestinians by the United States and Israel.

July 23, 1997, Washington.   Three members of an antigovernment militia were convicted in a string of bank robberies and bombings that prosecutors called domestic terrorism. On April 1, 1996, the terrorists, dressed in military-style camouflage, robbed the U.S. Bank in Spokane, Washington. As a diversion, the group detonated a bomb at the *Spokane Review* newspaper office a few minutes before the robbery. On July 12, 1996, the group bombed a Planned Parenthood office and then robbed the same bank branch again. About $108,000 taken in the robberies was never recovered. The militiamen consider themselves "Ambassadors of Yahweh," a form of the Hebrew name for God in the Old Testament, and believe northern Europeans are the true Israelites. One of the terrorists was a former nuclear power plant engineer and another was a former supervisor for AT&T.

July 31, 1997, New York.   Police raided a Brooklyn apartment and arrested two Palestinian men who were allegedly planning suicide bombings of a busy subway and a commuter bus. Both suspects were wounded when they lunged for explosive devices. Authorities discovered powerful pipe bombs made with gunpowder, nails, and toggle switches; reams of political literature attacking Israel; and a portrait of Sheik

Omar Abdul Rahman, a militant Egyptian cleric who plotted to bomb the United Nations and other New York landmarks.

December 2, 1997, Florida. Fugitive Ramon Aldasoro Magunacelaya, a suspected Basque terrorist wanted in Spain for murdering a Spanish general and two police officers, was arrested by the FBI. Spanish prosecutors said that Aldasoro was a member of the ETA (Basque Fatherland and Liberty) terrorist organization that has killed about 800 people. Aldasoro, the first Basque terrorist to be arrested in the United States, had been working as a Toyota salesman at the time of his arrest. A police officer who issued a traffic citation to Aldasoro in 1996 did not know he had stopped a wanted terrorist; Aldasoro had obtained a phony Florida driver's license.

December 12, 1997, Arkansas. Three white supremacists, who wanted to create the Aryan People's Republic, were charged with planning to revolt against the government by kidnapping and killing police and public officials. One of the terrorists, a forty-year-old man from Idaho, murdered a man he believed was a federal informer. The other two men robbed a gun dealer in Tilly, Arkansas, to obtain weapons for their cause, murdered three people, and were allegedly involved in a shootout with Ohio police. Once the government was gone, the group planned to recruit certain white people with the Republic and then engage in polygamy so that the number of recruits would increase.

January 29, 1998, Alabama. The Army of God claimed credit for a bombing at the New Woman, All Women Health Care Clinic, that killed Robert D. Sanderson, a thirty-five-year-old Birmingham police officer, and wounded nurse Emily Lyons, who lost her left eye and suffered serious injuries to her legs and abdomen. Officer Sanderson was the sixth person to die from violence at abortion clinics since 1993. Dr. David Gunn was murdered in Florida by Michael Griffith, an abortion protestor, in March 1993. On July 29, 1994, also in Florida, Dr. John Britton and his security escort, James Barrett, were shot to death by Paul Hill, another protestor. In Massachusetts on December 30, 1994, John Salvi opened fired in two clinics, killing receptionists Lee Ann Nichols and Shannon Lowney and wounding five other people. On August 19, 1993, in Wichita, Kansas, Rachelle Shannon shot and wounded Dr. George Tiller in both arms in the parking lot of his clinic.

February 19, 1998, Nevada.   FBI agents arrested Larry Wayne Harris, a microbiologist and former member of the Aryan Nations, and microbiologist William Leavitt, Jr., and charged them with possessing the deadly biological agent anthrax. Harris reportedly boasted he had enough of the substance to "wipe out the city" of Las Vegas. The government affidavit noted that in 1997 Harris told an unidentified group of his plans to place bubonic plague toxin in a New York City subway station where it would cause hundreds of thousands of deaths that would be blamed on the Iraqi government. (A laboratory in Maryland had sent Harris three vials of bubonic plague bacteria through the mail in 1995.) On February 22, 1998, authorities concluded that the seized vials contained harmless anthrax vaccine that was not a threat to public safety.

Index

Index